'In this evocative, witty, candid and instructi[...]
demanding experience of working in an ED [...]
recount her daily experiences in a manner tha[...]
and profoundly moving. In sharing her personal thoughts and observations, she
demonstrates the reflective capacity and emotional generosity required to navigate
working in this highly charged context, in which wrestling with "Grim" is an
everyday occurrence. We can all learn something important about managing stress
and trauma from her words.'
– PROFESSOR GILLIAN EAGLE, PROFESSOR OF PSYCHOLOGY AT THE UNIVERSITY OF
THE WITWATERSRAND AND AN EXPERIENCED CLINICAL PSYCHOLOGIST SPECIALISING
IN THE FIELD OF TRAUMATIC STRESS

'A rare and intimate insight into the thoughts and experiences of an ED doctor
and her responses to the idiosyncratic cast of characters that she meets. The book
speaks movingly to the author's life outside of her work. Written in the time of the
Corona pandemic, it extends well beyond this. A deeply ironic, humorous and yet
compassionate book. A must read.'
– GILLIAN STRAKER, CLINICAL PROFESSOR, UNIVERSITY OF SYDNEY AND CO-
AUTHOR OF THE TALKING CURE

'What a riveting read. I couldn't put it down!'
– PROFESSOR MARK BUSSIN

'Brilliant! Such an epic representation of life in the ED.'
– FEROZA MOTARA, ACADEMIC HEAD: EMERGENCY MEDICINE, THE UNIVERSITY
OF THE WITWATERSRAND AND HEAD: ED, CMJAH

'Intriguing, with a wicked sense of humour, this book captured my imagination. A
glimpse of a frontline worker during the COVID-19 pandemic. A must read!'
– MICHAEL WALDECK, HEAD, WILGEHEUWEL EMERGENCY DEPARTMENT

'Anne sheds light on life on the frontline in this candid, humorous and tremendously
entertaining compilation of some of her career highlights and memories. This book
is the collective experience of a fabulous clinician and an amazing human being. If
only there were more pages.'
– PROFESSOR ZEYN MAHOMED, HEAD: EMERGENCY DEPARTMENT, CHRIS HANI
BARAGWANATH ACADEMIC HOSPITAL

Saving a Stranger's Life

Saving a Stranger's Life

The diary of an emergency room doctor

ANNE BICCARD

Published in by Jacana Media (Pty) Ltd in 2020
Second impression 2021
Third impression 2022
Fourth impression 2023

10 Orange Street
Sunnyside
Auckland Park 2092
South Africa
+2711 628 3200
www.jacana.co.za

© Anne Biccard, 2020

ISBN 978-1-4313-3065-9

Cover design publicide
Design and layout by Shawn Paikin
Editing by Michele Magwood
Proofreading by Lara Jacob
Set in Ehrhardt 12/16pt
Printed by Creda Communications, Cape Town
Job no. 003727

For a complete list of Jacana titles visit
www.jacana.co.za

Preface

The Emergency Department of a hospital is a tense place to work even without a pandemic on the loose. Add in the deadly coronavirus and your day-to-day work becomes terrifying.

This is a frontline account of working in an ED in South Africa as we face an evolving horror. We are seeing the desperately ill and the 'worried well' and many more in between. The tales that follow are based on real-life events and show that fact is often stranger than fiction.

I write in the present tense because work in the ED is real-time. Of course, hindsight is 20/20 and, with the benefit of tomorrow's knowledge, every story would tell itself differently.

None of us knows what tomorrow will bring. These terrible times are in their infancy and there are plenty of surprises to come. My story is told as our experience unfolds and our understanding of Covid-19 evolves.

I hope to reach some kind of conclusion, but I am not sure what that end will look like.

This book is dedicated to all my colleagues, medical and paramedical, who have selflessly kept coming to work despite the grave personal risk posed by the pandemic.

We are masked and gloved warriors, all over the world, facing the flood of sick patients daily and keeping up a professional service despite a real and present danger.

Many of these healthcare workers will not live to read the tales of their bravery. This book is dedicated to the truly special people who purposefully put themselves in the line of fire, day and night, in order to save a stranger's life.

One

We are in the thick of the panic about the coronavirus. Everyone in the Emergency Department is wearing masks and gowns and it feels like the apocalypse has arrived. We are using gloves to examine the patients, but then touching the telephones and doors and countertops with our gloved hands and so the virus is probably everywhere already. We don't want to throw away protective equipment because we know that the supply is limited, and we don't know how long this crisis will last.

The ED has become a war zone and life, as we know it, is forever changed. All this chaos stems from a germ with a little halo, which looks like a crown, and is accordingly named Coronavirus.

South Africa has the first confirmed case today. It happens to be my birthday.

It feels like nature is taking revenge on the human race, and perhaps it is. I can't help thinking that we have somehow brought this on ourselves. I am reminded that 'it's natural' is a phrase used for comfort and solace, but nature is not always a reassuring thing. Nature can be howlingly powerful and destructive. Tsunamis and hurricanes leave a wake of devastation wider than most 'unnatural' events could ever cause.

I am hoping that the virus will be slightly attenuated by its travel across the globe and that we will not see the high rates of serious disease that have wracked the northern hemisphere. Our healthcare

1

system does not have the capacity to cope and it will collapse like a house of cards.

I am googling how many ventilated beds we have in Gauteng when the sister on duty calls me for a patient who has been triaged as orange. This means that the patient must be seen immediately.

Triage is a system of ordering the patients according to urgency. The term originated in Napoleonic times when the war wounded were sorted in terms of priority, and now there is an internationally accepted protocol to try and reduce the risk of seriously ill patients being made to wait while less urgent patients are attended to.

We now have two streams of triage: one for patients who might have coronavirus and one for all the rest. We are trying to limit exposure to the virus and a nurse at the front door is asking for symptoms and travel history. Of course, the criteria for travel history changes every day as the new cases are clocked around the world. Initially it was China only, then it increased to include 7 more countries and then 11.

Today there are more than 20 countries on the list, and I decide to stop calling the help line for an update. There is just a recorded message now, directing us to consult their website.

Aside from the queue of possible coronas, the usual suspects are still coming through the ED. I pick up the next file marked 'Orange' – for very urgent - and I see the complaint is vaginal bleeding. I sigh internally. Vaginal bleeding is a common complaint and, try as I might, I cannot seem to prevent these patients being whisked through ahead of all others. Perhaps it is the dangerous mystery of it all, bleeding from an invisible place.

Any bleeding that is life-threatening must be prioritised above most other patients. A serious hemorrhage will be seen ahead of everyone else aside, perhaps, from a choking person. It would depend on whether the choking person is moving air at all. This is the difficulty of triage, as it is not always easy to separate the seriously ill from the people who think that they should be seen immediately.

It would be very unusual for a vaginal bleed to be life-threatening but at least the patient is unlikely to expose me to the coronavirus. When I get to the bed, however, I see that this young woman is really bleeding. Her dress and the linen are soaked through and the blood is clotting on the bed.

Her mother stands angrily next to her, glaring at me, as though I am somehow the offender. The young lady looks stricken and is trying to appear nonchalant, as only a teenager can.

'Is there any possibility that you could be pregnant?' I ask, glancing at her age on the sticker.

Thirteen. A bit young, but possible.

'No.' Her eyes dart up and to the right as she answers. A classic tell that she is lying.

'Let's do urine just to check.' I suggest diplomatically.

'There is absolutely no possibility that she is pregnant.' Mom looks more annoyed. My attempt to get urine is thwarted for now; I will ask her again when the mom is out of the room.

'OK, let's have a look," I nod towards the door. 'Perhaps you could wait outside while I examine her?'

Mom's answer is unequivocal and snappy.

'No.'

I can't make her mother go outside so I go ahead and cover the patient with a towel and ask her to take her panties off. When I lift the towel to examine her, I see she has waxed off all her pubic hair except for a thin strip in the middle. A Brazilian wax. The nurse's eyebrows shoot up.

'Hierdie punda is gebruik,' she uses Afrikaans as a disguise. Roughly translated, it means 'this vagina is in use'. I couldn't agree more. I need to sneak a pregnancy test past mom. An idea bobs to the surface of my consciousness. I open a pregnancy test and dip the end into the blood on the bed in the same way that one would do with urine. The absorbent material draws the serum up and one stripe appears. As it migrates higher, a second stripe appears.

Positive.

Now it is imperative to get Mom out of the room. She is young but has the yellowed fingers and lined face of a heavy smoker. I saunter off with a casual 'back in a moment' and write some scripts for other patients. I make a few calls and check the internet news on the pandemic.

Sure enough, a few minutes later I see Mom heading for the doors, fumbling in her handbag for her cigarettes. 'Gotcha.' I smile to myself and nip into the cubicle.

When I tell the young lady that she is pregnant, she doesn't look at all surprised. She has probably already done a test at home. But she refuses to let me tell her mother. 'She'll kill me. She got pregnant at 15 with my brother. I'd rather die than tell her.'

The apple doesn't fall far from the tree, I think. I tell her that we have no choice but to inform her mother as the law requires her mother's permission for any surgical treatment. 'I would rather die' is a figure of speech which might well apply here if we don't stop the bleeding.

While we are arguing, the mom returns to the room. The sudden silence is almost comical, but she seems not to notice. She stands in the doorway with her hands on her hips, staring at us. We stare guiltily back.

I decide to make it the gynaecologist's problem. She will need to do an ultrasound to exclude an ectopic pregnancy and take it from there. At the very least the patient will need a D and C. Bleeding this heavy is either an ectopic pregnancy, which I am suspecting, or a miscarriage. I excuse myself and leave the two in deafening silence. I am amazed that Mom does not follow me with questions, but perhaps she thinks we are no further along the diagnostic pathway. The ED is busy; all the cubicles are full, and I need to move on.

Two

Last night the president gave a speech and declared a state of disaster. Ports of entry are being closed and travel visas cancelled. Anyone with overseas travel history must present themselves for screening.

There is a queue of people winding through the parking lot, presenting themselves. They anticipate being tested for the virus, but we are screening them in order to decide whether they qualify to have the test. No one seems to understand the difference between screening and testing, and I feel that my sanity is quivering at its roots. During the screening, we ask if the patient has travelled to a high-risk area or had contact with a corona-positive person and if they have symptoms. They must answer yes to both questions in order to test.

Tempers are frayed. A young man with a sore throat glares at me resentfully. He has not travelled but he heard that someone at his workplace may have been positive. I explain that this does not fit the criteria for coronavirus testing.

'Well, I'm here to get the test.' He looks at me like I am a pesky obstacle to overcome.

'You don't qualify for a test because you have no travel history and have had no definite contact with anyone with the virus.'

'But I want to get the test. I have paid for it.'

No 'out-loud' voice, I remind myself.

Instead of telling him what I think, I calmly explain to him that he has come for screening, not testing, and that he has paid for consultation, not testing. The result of the consultation is that he does not need to be tested. If everyone in the country with a sore throat had a swab for the virus, the test kits would be finished, and the labs swamped.

He is not interested. He doesn't care that there is a protocol and that we must be rational in the face of a potential national health crisis. There are limited resources and we need to allocate them accordingly.

He is furious that I will not bend on this issue. I examine him and send him on his way with a script. He says that he is not leaving until he gets the test. I tell him that he will be here for a long time then, as we won't be doing the test on him in the near future. He glares at me like an angry wasp for five minutes, while I start with the next patient, and then storms out.

I can see a complaint looming, but I am too tired to care.

I glance at my phone and see an urgent message from the laboratory that they are running out of the reagent used for running the test and requesting that we stick to the guidelines and not test people unnecessarily. I feel bad as I have made two exceptions to the rule today – one for a lady who works in a kiosk at the airport and one for a taxi driver dedicated to the airport run. Neither had a definite positive contact nor a travel history but they had contact with hundreds of international travellers over the past month. They both had symptoms of a viral infection and elderly parents living with them. I swabbed them both and sent them home to self-isolate. At least I didn't get bullied into an unnecessary test for The Angry Wasp.

The guy in the cubicle next door is vomiting for the first team. Initially I am not sure if he is shouting or retching, but it sounds like he is being exorcised.

'Put up a drip!' I call to the sister through the curtain. 'Give odansetron if there are no allergies.' The drug is a powerful anti-nausea treatment and should work quickly.

In a perverse moment I push the voice record function on my mobile and make a sound clip of the vomiting, which I may later use as a ringtone.

I finish my current consultation and go into the cubicle. The vomiter is crouching on the floor with his arms stretched out in front of him. He looks like he is doing yoga with his head under the bed. I lean down so that I can make eye contact.

'Hello.'

He shakes his head and vomits some more. He tries to aim for the wastepaper basket but fails.

'Can you get up on the bed so that we can put up a drip?'

He shakes his head again. He is drenched in sweat. I presume the sister has gone to get medication as there is no one in sight. I tell him to stay on the floor until he feels less nauseous. I trot off to get some odansetron and kneel behind him. I pull down his pants and give him a shot in the buttock.

When I come back later, he is still vomiting, although less violently. The sisters have reappeared, got him onto the bed, and put up a drip. They have also given him a bowl sheathed in a plastic bag. He clutches it like a drowning man.

'So. You are vomiting.' I state the obvious. After a few questions I narrow the possibilities down to a kidney stone or a bowel obstruction. He is 61 years of age with severe abdominal pain, nausea and vomiting which started about an hour ago.

On examination, his abdomen is tight as a drum and what is termed 'exquisitely tender'. I learned this surgical term from the professor of surgery who trained me, although my pronunciation of 'exquisite' could never match her posh tone. Such a tender abdomen tells me that he is unlikely to have a kidney stone. The pain from kidney stones is not elicited by pressing on the stomach because the kidneys are retroperitoneal, which means that they lie behind the abdominal cavity. The abdominal X-ray confirms a bowel obstruction. Multiple air–fluid levels, like flat-bottomed clouds, are scattered throughout the image.

The vomiter has deteriorated while having the X-ray. His level of consciousness has dropped and now he is barely rousable. It may be that we have given him too much medication for pain and vomiting, or the bowel obstruction is longer standing than I thought. As I speak to the family, he starts to vomit dark brown liquid. It is spurting out of his mouth like a fountain and I quickly turn him on his side.

'Suction!' I call out to anyone within earshot. I am standing next to the bed, holding his shoulder so that he remains lateral, and trying to keep my feet out of the way.

'Hold him here!' I tell an alarmed-looking son. I put on gloves and connect the suction catheter to the wall unit. Two sisters have arrived to help, and they roll him on to his back and lift the head of the bed. I start to suction the airway, but he has already inhaled a fair amount of stomach contents. Each breath makes a hideous gurgling sound.

Now the vomit is pure faeces. Stool from his blocked bowel shoots out of his mouth and I can't clear it with the suction. Particulate matter is stuck in the catheter tip and, even with repeated wiping, the suction is blocked. The dark brown, lumpy fluid continues to gush up and now I am struggling not to vomit myself. I swallow against the retching and wipe my face on my sleeve as I hold his airway open. Sweat runs down my neck.

This resuscitation, or 'resus' as we say, reminds me of doing a rotation in forensic pathology when I was a student. Blocking my nose with menthol rub, mouth-breathing and wearing a heavy scarf over the lower half of my face couldn't save me from the smell. The mortuary was full of gruesome surprises, and I just could not get used to the stench of rotting bodies.

Finally, I manage to clear the vomiter's airway and get him stable enough to send to the ward. He is intubated and needs to go back for another X-ray to check for aspiration pneumonia. In a bowel obstruction, the fluid and faeces cannot get past the blockage and so they are regurgitated backwards to the stomach. This results in enthusiastic vomiting and a semi-conscious patient taking a deep breath can inhale the vomitus. Aspiration pneumonia is like drowning in your own digestive products, except the lung does a lot less well with the acidotic, particulate matter than it would with plain old water.

I am still feeling queasy and need to stand outside in the sunshine for a full five minutes before I can stomach another patient.

Three

Hospital management is scrambling to keep ahead of the coming plague. The first sign was the gazebo outside the ED. Initially it was intended for staff to just hand out information leaflets and spray patients' hands, but it then turned into a full triage system, filtering the patients with respiratory symptoms to one side in order to minimise cross-contamination.

Today the gazebo has been replaced with a small tent. There are masked staff directing patients and spraying them down with chlorhexidine mixture, a strong antiseptic solution that seems to kill most known viruses and bacteria.

I put my mobile phone on silent because it pings every second with new messages and protocols from groups and government agencies and fellow doctors. Everyone is trying to be prepared and none of us really know what we are preparing for.

I wish that I could go home and stay there for six months. There is no chance of that, though, so I might as well resign myself to getting Covid at some point. I hope that my immune system is strong enough to beat it; or at least clever enough not to go on the rampant destruction of lung tissue that seems to happen about 10 days into the infection.

It is not yet 6 am when the blare of a car horn outside the double doors jars us all. A lady is slumped in the passenger seat and the driver leans on the hooter before rushing around to open her door. I snatch a few sets of gloves and a stretcher. The little wheels bump over the uneven bricks and I spot a sinister stain on the paving. Smokers huddle around the concrete ashtray next to the ambulance bay. As the passenger door swings open, the lady falls forward and a stream of vomit splatters the paving. I step back smartly, avoiding the pungent bile.

The lady doesn't look good. Nausea and vomiting can cause pallor, but this lady is an alarming shade of greyish blue. We heft her awkwardly out of the seat, onto the stretcher and she is raced into the ED. I hang back, asking the driver for some history.

'She works for me, I don't really know her medical history,' he tells me, flustered. 'She hasn't been feeling well the past few days. Short of breath, maybe some chest pain.'

I wonder what she was doing at work before 6 am but decide not to ask. I do ask, however, if she had influenza-like symptoms, a fever or a travel history. The answer is no to all three.

'Doctor!' The nurse holds the door open, calling me into the resuscitation bay. There is a way in which nurses call doctors when there is trouble afoot. I suspect that this is a universal thing. If the patient becomes unstable, or is actively caught in the act of dying, the nurse will summon the doctor in a particular tone. The tone says 'hurry'. I did.

Passenger lady is in cardiac arrest.

I am relieved that there is no history suggestive of coronavirus as I hear that cardiopulmonary resuscitation – CPR for short – on an infected individual is a sure-fire way to get sick.

Emergency medicine is very protocol driven. Most situations have a mnemonic or algorithm to follow, a reassuring map for the panicking mind. The algorithm for cardiac arrest flashes through my mind as we start CPR on passenger lady.

I take my place at the head of the bed and put a breathing mask over her nose and mouth. I glance at the clock. It is almost 6.30 am; the new shift takes over at 7 am. It is a great pity that I cannot make this their problem. I hold up her chin to keep her airway open and squeeze the bag. It makes a sad, rhythmical groan. One of the sisters presses on the chest for 30 cycles then I get to breathe twice.

It is not easy to blow air into the chest at the same time as someone else is compressing the chest wall. Mostly, the air comes shooting back, bringing saliva, stomach contents and dentures with it.

Early in the science of CPR, we divided up the breaths and the compressions so that each could enjoy independent efficacy. At present 30 compressions are answered by two breaths; sort of like a formalised prayer. Over the years, different ratios have been tried. There is currently a proposal to the Resuscitation Council that we move away from the whole idea of ventilation and rely on the movement of the chest wall during compressions to move the air. It certainly would make CPR easier and less intimate for members of the public to perform

We are pumping and oxygenating while I try to figure out what is going on with this lady. She doesn't look old or chronically ill.

The mnemonic to remind me of the possible causes for sudden cardiac arrest is 'Hs and Ts'. There are six of each. I run through them in my head as a dexterous nurse finds a vein and inserts an IV. The lab technician has magically appeared and takes blood from the IV site.

The first H is hypovolemia. Massive blood loss can lead to low fluid volume and make the heart stop. That doesn't really fit with the history of shortness of breath but could fit with chest pain if she had a ruptured aortic aneurysm. Now she has no recordable blood pressure on the monitor but that is probably because her heart has stopped, rather than the other way around. It doesn't jump out at me as the probable cause.

Next, hypoxia. Low oxygenation. No, her airway was open when she arrived. Unless there is a problem with oxygenation on a cellular level, like cyanide poisoning, which seems highly unlikely. Leaving that one behind I move to the next three Hs. Hydrogen ions or acidosis, and hyper- or hypo-kalaemia. Potassium is very tightly regulated in the blood and a peak or a dip can stop the heart

13

instantaneously. We need to check the blood potassium level.

The next H stands for hypothermia, but she doesn't feel cold. I race through them, but my mind is already set on one of the Ts. Doubling back, I ask one of the nurses to check the sugar level. Hypoglycaemia, or low blood sugar, is the last H.

Definitely, a T is to blame. Six Hs. Six Ts. The first T is tablets or toxins. Where has the driver of the car gone anyway? In the short term, history is vital if one is to catch a toxin as the culprit. Blood results take too long, and you must have an idea of what you are looking for.

The algorithm for finding a toxin is the seven Ps, representing the seven places to check for clues of poison or drug ingestion on an unconscious patient. Check pupils, look for pinpricks, search pockets, quiz parents, peers and partners and do a toxicology screen on their pee. I think that avenue is a dead end, so to speak. I am suspecting one of the other Ts. Thromboembolism to the lung or thrombosis to the heart. It is almost impossible to tell these siblings apart at this late stage of the game. Either way, we give her a solid jolt of adrenaline in the IV, but her skin remains mottled and icy. We are 15 minutes into CPR, and I feel a slow dread and inexorable tiredness creeping up.

I sometimes joke with my colleagues about the Grim Reaper. I call him Grim, rather than Mr Reaper. It's a deliberate attempt to both familiarise and shun him. No one can work in an ED without forming some kind of relationship with him. I see him as an adversary and, for some reason, I see him as male. Either way, Grim has a firm grasp on Passenger Lady, but I am also holding fast. The tussle that awaits us all – sometimes professionally and always personally.

Grim always wins in the end, of course, but it is really pleasing to get a point on the board every now and again.

Passenger lady's arm bounces lifelessly with each chest compression. I squeeze the bag to ventilate her. Sugar level is normal, blood gas shows acidosis. Again, I think, the result of the arrest, rather than the cause. Anyone who is not breathing adequately will become acidotic because, in the absence of oxygen, the cells make lactic acid.

The sister counting the cycles of CPR instructs a pause. There is, of course, an algorithm. Two minutes of chest compressions, then stop and check the patient. My hands are drenched with sweat inside the blue latex as I put the paddles on her chest to check for a rhythm. To my amazement, a tracing appears. Irregular, but there's a definite spike and dip on the monitor. The mood of the resus team lifts palpably.

We aren't out of the woods just yet as there can be electrical activity in the heart without an effective pumping action of the muscle. Called pulseless electrical activity, or PEA, it has been known to fool many a doctor too focused on the monitors and not on the patient. But I am an old dog and not that easily tricked. I feel her neck for a pulse. Right there, in the groove next to her trachea, I feel a rhythmic pumping under my fingertips.

Passenger Lady is making a comeback. I am one up on Grim.

Four

Tonight, our president is addressing the nation. He is rational and articulate, and I agree with everything that he says. Not that I get to watch the speech, as I am busy seeing patients, but my friends message me as they watch. The summary is that the country is going to be on lockdown for 21 days from Thursday. Businesses will be closed and non-essential travel is banned.

Sadly for me, I am essential, and I will keep working, like a sacrificial lamb, until something radical changes.

Our little band of doctors and nurses watch the tide of people over the tops of our masks. It feels inevitable that we will all get sick and it doesn't feel like we have any agency in this wave of madness. It is roasting hot under the personal protective equipment, or PPE, and a constant trickle of sweat streams off my forehead. I feel like I might burst into flames at any moment. I cannot hear what the patients are saying to me and they cannot hear me either. We shout at each other through layers of plastic.

The emotional climate in South Africa is interesting. After the rocky political ride over the past 60 years, I think that we are as jaded as we can be. The overriding sentiment is amazement that anything other than trickery is coming from the government. I am struck by how awed we all are that South Africa is finally getting something right. I reflect that, as a country, we have an extremely poor sense of self-esteem.

This is the first crisis in which people are not emigrating en masse. The first time that we are huddled together, regardless of race, and facing a global timebomb. We are all amazed that our president actually seems to have taken good advice, can make a speech which is sensible in any way, and ends with such a genuine plea for God to bless Africa that even I have tears in my eyes. When I finally hear the address, that is, which is two days later on YouTube.

I have spent the last two days at work, aside from six hours when I slept like the dead. A bad analogy, I think, as who knows where we will be six months from here. For all I know, the human race could be wiped out by this pandemic. Maybe this is what happened to the dinosaurs.

Sadly, death is an option for us all. Grim is having a field day, especially in Italy, where I hear that they are using ice rinks as emergency mortuaries.

I am reflecting on this depressing situation when I see that the Angry Wasp is back. I hear him telling the nurse in triage that his sore throat is not resolving and now he is sure that someone at his place of work has tested positive. She brings him through, resplendent in a home-crafted gas mask. Wearily, I pull the mobile table towards me and start to write the history. When I get to the part about a colleague being positive, I ask for the positive contact's name.

'What?' the Wasp asks. He stutters and stammers into his mask. 'I don't feel comfortable telling you that information.' He is making this up as he goes along, and I am having none of it.

'I'm afraid that coronavirus is a notifiable disease. Which means that the National Institute for Communicable Diseases is tracking all cases. So, all the positive people are on a database and they are tracking the spread and epidemiology every day.' I pause, my pen hovering above the notes as I wait for the name. I am also making this up as I go, but it seems plausible to me.

'I don't know his name,' The Wasp concedes. 'But he works in my building and I got an email.'

'So, you don't even know the name of the person or where exactly he works, but you got an email that someone in your company has tested positive?'

'Yes,' he bristles. His face is flushed with anger because he can see where I am going with this.

'I'm afraid that doesn't qualify as close contact.' I shake my head. He looks like he wants to throttle me. It would be easier to just do the test, but it has become a matter of principle to me.

The Angry Wasp is not getting tested.

The next patient, however, will be getting a test. He was in a hotel in China which had three confirmed cases. The hotel was quarantined for a full six weeks. In the dead of night, this guy found a fire door that was unlocked; he took his passport and wallet and hailed a taxi to the airport. When he arrived in South Africa, he developed a high fever and a raging sore throat.

He feels deeply sorry for himself.

I am at a bit of a loss of what to say. He is at risk of having the virus and giving it to the people around him. Exposure to illness is an inescapable part of medicine. The horrors of coronavirus may one day pale into insignificance when compared to bacterial meningitis or multi-drug resistant tuberculosis, but only time will tell. Right now, it seems like a pretty powerful germ.

I am told that more people have died from starvation than from Covid-19 so far this year in Africa. The difference is that poverty and starvation are not, strictly speaking, contagious. Outside of the cycle of unemployment, crime and poor self-esteem, that is. Anyone can get a virus; they are mysterious and diabolical and can evoke violent paranoia.

I have always been famously level-headed and even I am feeling paranoid.

Humans have imagination and so we fear 'what's out there', the invisible threat of a deadly poison in the air. I have a mental image of our ancestors, huddled in a cave, listening to the sound of a predator in the night, as sinister as the coughs and groans in the ED.

People are buying up toilet paper so that, when retail business grinds to a halt, they will still be able to wipe. They anticipate remaining isolated for months on end, eating baked beans and tinned sardines, but at least they will have toilet paper.

I tell Mr Absconder that he needs to take the business of self-isolation very seriously; we will swab him today and again in two weeks.

Being a healthcare worker with the coronavirus looming large is like working in the shadow of a nuclear blast. Aside from the frenzy of telephone enquiries and patients requesting testing, there are all the usual customers in the ED. Broken arms, seizures and sick babies; they are piling up in the triage area. We have no beds and the patients are sitting in the corridor and on the desks and wheelchairs. At least most of them have the sense to see that the unit is in crisis. Some of the less serious cases even go home without being seen, for which I am profoundly grateful.

If this epidemic continues to explode, I am going to develop a pressure sore on my nose from my tight mask.

The patient in bed three is a real misery. She is full of aches and pains and non-specific symptoms. Her extended family clusters around the bed, looking concerned. She hasn't eaten or had any fluid for weeks, they tell me. How many weeks, exactly, I ask, feigning attention to detail. A few, they assure me.

'More than two weeks?' I ask meticulously.

Definitely more than two weeks, they reply. I resist the impulse to roll my eyes. If she had not had anything to eat or drink for more than two weeks, she would be showing some visible sights of strain. Her tongue would be dry, her eyes sunken. But she looked sprightly and bright, following the interaction carefully and interjecting any forgotten fact.

Miraculously, her blood results and X-rays are normal. Her urine is clear. I cannot find anything wrong with her on examination. But she doesn't want to go home, and her family doesn't want to take her. Aside from her insistence that she needs to be hospitalised, there is no justification to keep her in.

She has her suitcase packed and ready.

She expects admission. In fact, her family demands it. They cannot take her home in this state, they tell me earnestly. I want to ask them what state, exactly, that is. It is the Thursday before a lockdown weekend and I suspect that the family wants to leave her here with us as a matter of convenience. Aside from visible wilting, I can find no objective evidence of illness. It is trying, to say the least, but I can see there is no escaping trying to refer her in.

Some physicians will just take the patient. Others will spend half an hour arguing and resisting. Some downright refuse to entertain the notion of admitting anyone unless they are objectively at death's door. In a way, the hard-sell physicians are easier; they just say no, rather than drawing out the agony. If I disagree, I will fight for the patient. But I would accept a straight 'no' on The Misery as I feel that this is an unnecessary referral anyway. The physician on call today is an arguer. I have wanted to tell him in the past that he could have already seen the patient in the time spent on negotiations; and, if he just saw the patient, he would at least get paid for his time. He is always moaning about how busy he is, but he would have a lot more time if he spent less of it trying to avoid the inevitable.

I brace myself and call him. I know that he will give me a speech about scarce resources in this pandemic.

'I have this lady in the ED,' I begin, 'with a positive suitcase sign.'

There is an astounded silence and then he laughs. It is a very unusual sound, like a donkey braying. I realise that, in 20 years of working with him, I have never heard him laugh. He is always in a hurry, his brows knitted and his body humming with stress. It can't be pleasant to take yourself so seriously and I feel a bit sorry for him. I will feel sorrier for him once he has consulted with The Misery and her miserable family and he realises that he is saddled with her miserableness for the whole weekend. If my suspicions are

21

correct, the hand-wringing family will only reappear on Tuesday.

I finally convince him to take her and now I must rustle up a credible diagnosis to put on the admission form that will get medical aid approval. I cannot call it dehydration because, despite not eating for weeks, her blood results are completely normal. I toy with anorexia or failure to thrive, but I am fairly sure medical aid will reject that. I look back over my notes and settle on general body weakness. I'm sure it will be sent back as it is more a description than a diagnosis, but I will give it a try.

When I go back to the bedside, the family has evaporated, and the patient asks me for water. It seems that she is going to break her fast. I fetch her a polystyrene cup and fill it with water from the tap. She looks at it distastefully.

'Don't you have any bottled water?' She asks. 'With this virus and all…'

'We aren't really in the catering business,' I reply smoothly and place the cup within reach. This lady has taken up way too much of my time already.

I am rescued by a priority one patient bellowing for help in the resuscitation room. An ambulance crew is loading him across from the stretcher to the bed, and the blood is cascading off the edge of the stretcher. He is on a canvas sheet with handles sewn into the sides and, where the material folds, it makes a funnel. I am accustomed to seeing spots of blood on the ED floor, but this is an unbroken trail of blood all the way from the ambulance bay. The patients' trouser leg is in tatters and I cut the remains off with a trauma scissors. These are like super sharp pruning scissors without sharp ends. Perfect for quickly cutting off clothing even if it is motorcycle leathers or denims. They have a flat plate on the bottom jaw to ensure that you don't take little nips out of the underlying patient.

His femur is shattered, there is a gaping hole in his upper leg with shards of bone gleaming white in the scarlet mess.

'What happened?' I ask the paramedic.

'He's a mechanic and was tightening the head on a compressor. The bolts weren't tight enough so when the pressure built up, the cylinder head flew off. Hit him straight on the leg.'

This is like an injury from a cannonball, I think. I am worried that he is bleeding from his femoral artery. There is not much room above the wound, but I manage to get a tourniquet around the top of the leg and tighten it as much as I can.

The blood keeps welling up and spilling onto the stretcher.

I can feel the first shiver of panic in my spine. I can't tighten the tourniquet anymore and the guy is just bleeding past it. I put up two big-bore intravenous lines and push fluids, then I pack wet gauze into the wound and elevate the foot of the bed.

I speed-dial the orthopaedic surgeon. Luckily, he is in the hospital and, within a few minutes, he is with me in the ED. He looks as worried as I feel, and we wheel the patient down to X-rays for an urgent CT angiogram. The radiologist will inject dye into his drip, which travels throughout the vascular system so that he can check if there are any leaks. The milky dye, or contrast, should stay in the arteries and veins. A cloudy billowing out of contrast into the tissues will tell us where the artery or vein is disrupted. If he is bleeding from an artery, we will need a vascular surgeon to repair it.

We do not have a vascular surgeon at this hospital.

Mercifully, the angiogram shows that he is bleeding from the broken bone and the network of veins around it. The orthopod can fix it and we rush the patient straight from X-rays into the theatre.

I am sweating and slightly elated with relief as I hand him over to the anaesthetist.

The young doctor who I am working with today does calligraphy in his spare time and writes beautiful notes with a fountain pen. He blows carefully on each sentence after completing it and has an array of pens lined up in the pocket of his scrubs. His notes are a work of art and I feel desperately inadequate when I compare my hasty scrawl. He did not see the cannonball patient and looks suspiciously at my blood-spattered shoes when I return to the ED.

He loves action and I feel like I have been cheating on him, seeing a trauma case without him. He was in the coffee shop and missed the whole thing. He was getting his last energy drink before the cafeteria closes for three long weeks; I am not sure how he will cope without them.

Guidelines state that only essential services and retail will be available. I wonder if energy drinks will qualify. It seems that alcohol and cigarettes are not essential, and their sale will be banned. I wonder how that will pan out for us.

I suggest that my colleague might like to see the next patient who has chest pain, but he declines as he still has to discharge about 10 people. And he must blow all the notes dry as he goes. I pick up the electrocardiogram, or ECG, on the way to the bed and notice some old changes. The ECG is a recording of the heart muscle's electrical activity. Each part of the heartbeat should be represented by a deflection or wave on the monitor. If some of the heart tissue is running out of oxygen, or is already dead, it changes the shape of the waves in a characteristic fashion. The ECG also gives you information about irregular rhythms and other important parameters. Once you have had a heart attack, some changes on your ECG may become permanent.

I ask the patient if he has seen a cardiologist previously; I am hoping that there is an ECG somewhere in the system with which I can compare this one.

'Yes, Dr Jones here knows me well.'

Pleased, I carry the ECG off to the doctor's room and call Dr Jones. I know his speed code off by heart, like most of the specialists in the hospital, and it saves me a heap of time.

'Who did you say the patient is?' Dr Jones sounds suspicious.

I repeat the patient's name. The doctor is slightly incredulous. 'He said that I am his cardiologist?'

'Yes,' I reply. Dr Jones sounds like he doesn't like this guy much. Maybe he owes him money. But the conversation takes a different turn.

'Did he tell you that he tried to kill me?' Dr Jones asks.

'No!' I reply, horrified. 'How?'

'When he had his previous heart attack, he was admitted here in the ICU. He kept going outside to smoke and, at five in the morning, he signed himself out. The ICU staff called me at home to tell me and I rushed in to speak some sense to him. As I drove into the parking lot, I saw him getting into his car. He was still wearing his hospital gown. I parked and ran towards him, and, when he saw me, he accelerated directly at me. I had to jump into the agapanthus bed to avoid being killed. I am most certainly not his cardiologist.'

'Oh dear,' I reply. I go back to the patient.

'There seems to be a bit of a misunderstanding,' I say. 'Dr Jones is under the impression that you tried to kill him.'

The patient has the grace to look slightly embarrassed. 'Oh yes, that.' He says. 'I hoped that he had forgotten about it.'

I sink my head into my hands, then immediately jerk it back, remembering not to touch my face in fear of the virus. I wonder where I am going to find a cardiologist to see a patient with this abysmal history; attempted murder is harder to justify than outstanding debt.

Between the Misery, the Cannonball and the Assassin, I have been distracted from the virus for at least an hour. I had almost forgotten about it, but the queue of dejected, coughing people in masks is a harsh reminder. It is still there, and I fear it will be there for a good few months at least. Maybe it will loom large for the rest of life as we know it. I look at the clock. Still another four hours to go before the end of my shift. It feels like forever.

The number of infected people is 709 definite positives as of today. There are two critical patients on ventilators. Neither is in our hospital, but I am keeping an eye on their progress through the multiple networking groups that have sprung up over the past two weeks.

It is all overwhelming and depressing, like we are facing a long, relentless winter across the globe.

It feels like all the magic is gone.

Five

Today, Friday, is our first day of national lockdown. The number of those infected is around 1000 today. Three more are on ventilators

We wake up to the sad news of the first two deaths in South Africa.

We are warned that there will be roadblocks and no unnecessary travel will be allowed. I have my letter of appointment from the hospital, ready for any spot checks. But the streets are empty and there is a feeling of Armageddon in the city.

Visiting hours at the hospital have been suspended and the parking lot is empty. A lonely sister sits in the tent, her hand sanitiser ready. A few stragglers in masks are making their way towards her.

My shift is dragging by and I feel restless in the ED. There is a low rumble of thunder and I wander out into the hot, still afternoon. The air is sticky and electric with tension as white lightning flickers between the bulging bellies of clouds. I sit on the small wall outside the ED and watch the clouds bank higher until they block out the sun. The storm gathers in gusts and grumbles and the world seems suddenly threatening. Brilliant white adders of lightning twist towards the earth. A crack of thunder and the first fat drop slaps the ground. Another and another fall until the rain is a rush of applause. Petrichor fills my nostrils, the heady scent of rain drenching the thirsty earth. The stifling heat is broken, and the afternoon turns an ethereal green.

I wish that the rain would wash the world clean of this crazy contaminant. As it stands today, there are only four countries worldwide that have been spared from the coronavirus. I suspect that those countries are just not testing yet.

Four o'clock in the afternoon marks the end of my shift. If I hurry, I will be home in time to take the greyhounds for a walk before dark. Luckily, we live on a farm, so I can walk the dogs; under the lockdown rules, people are not allowed out into public spaces.

The roads are deserted again on my journey home. It feels so strange, like I am the last person on earth.

Five greyhounds fit into my long shadow as we make our way across the evening field. The other five wander in the tawny grass, sniffing for mice and messages. They cast their own shadows – matt versions of their lean and glossy bodies. The shadows stretch and wobble like Salvador Dali paintings in the slanting light.

Yes, there are 10 greyhounds. I seldom admit that I used to have 16. They are all rescue animals.

I wonder if Grim is like a shadow. We recognise him because he eclipses energy. He is an absence of light. Can death exist independently of what has died? Mulling this over, half of the walk passes without my noticing. I am trudging along, blind to the beauty around me. I put Grim out of my head. It is time to turn for home and I whistle to the dogs. The most recently adopted one hangs back with watchful, liquid eyes. He is pitch black with white splashes on the tips of his paws and tail. He is not quite sure of his new pack yet and his tail is always firmly between his muscular legs. It will take time, but he will learn to wag it.

I call them 'the snoopies' because of their big noses and long, whippy tails. Greyhounds are famous lovers of luxury and are either panting hot or curled up cold. Within seconds of wild running through the fields they sprawl, fast asleep, on the various cushions and carpets around the house.

Twilight spreads up the valley, golden light seeping into the creases and folds. Blues and greens merge in the honeyed light and tiny teams of insects hover in the air. Seams of shrubs give texture to the hazy quilt as the sharp edges of day blur into the blanket of night.

If I flew high enough, I think, I could hold the sunrise and sunset in the same lens. The humming heat is easing, and the air vibrates with frogs and crickets. They welcome the cool air and the long, dark swim through the night to come.

Our small house is set on a hillside, overlooking miles of patchwork farmland. In the daylight, the view of the valley is breathtaking. At night, the darkness is absolute, and the house is like an island in the black sea.

On some evenings I practise the cello or piano, but tonight I just feel like silence. Feet up, with a glass of wine in hand, I watch the night slowly descend. The frogs at the dam sound like race cars, revving and rasping. I wait for the day to recede and a slow heaviness to take me to bed.

I hope that I don't wake up with a sore throat or headache.

Six

A colleague keeps two pet warthogs. He calls me on Saturday morning to say the technician fixing his alarm has a laceration on his leg from one of the warthogs. Could I have a look – it will need to be cleaned and might need a stitch. Sure, I reply, send him in.

It is the second day of lockdown. I suppose that fixing an alarm is an essential service. The numbers on my WhatsApp groups confirm 1170 infections have been documented, and I see that the death toll is revised to one. The 28-year-old man who died in the Western Cape did not test positive for the virus, which is a good thing. On the other hand, Moody's has downgraded South Africa to junk status and the rand has fallen to a record low.

Just what we need to cheer us up.

To add to my misery, I receive a link on one of my groups with an update on ventilator settings for severe Covid-19 pneumonia. Once patients develop acute respiratory distress syndrome from pneumonia it seems that they have only a 10 per cent chance of survival. The link goes on to explain how one can, theoretically, ventilate four people on one ventilator.

What a dreadful thought. I am reminded of a dystopian novel that I read years ago called *The Road*, which was so profoundly bleak that it scarred me mentally and emotionally. Could Cormac McCarthy's depressing vision be coming true?

It turns out that the warthog victim is the wife of the technician.

The pet warthog – who weighs more than 100 kilograms – has been chasing the technician around all week. He is thin as a rail and quick on his feet, but his wife is not as agile. She got out of the bakkie while her husband was busy with the alarm and the warthog charged her. When I lift her culotte-type leggings, I find her whole inner thigh is hanging open.

I once saw a similar injury when a very overweight lady had been standing on the rim of the toilet. Her reasoning remains uncertain – perhaps she thought it more hygienic than sitting on the seat – but the bowl of the toilet broke under her significant weight. The edge of broken porcelain sliced through her flesh like a razor, splitting the back of her leg in half. I could literally put my fist right into the wound and the edges reached past my elbow.

The toilet bowl percher had not been on medical aid but at least the warthog victim is, so I can admit her to have the wound cleaned and sutured in theatre.

I call the orthopaedic surgeon to refer the patient. He seems confused as to why it needs to be closed in the theatre with intravenous antibiotics. Being Czechoslovakian, he might not know what a warthog is.

'The tusks are like teeth,' I explain. 'Little horns from the mouth. They get rubbed in soil and get food on them, so they are not very clean.'

'Ah,' I hear understanding in his voice. 'So. It is still inside?'

'Is what inside?'

'This... tisk.'

'No, no, the tusk is on the warthog. It is still on the warthog.'

'I come to see her.'

The phone goes dead and two minutes later the orthopod barrels into the casualty unit. He is a giant of a man who dresses in battle fatigues with half-moon spectacles hanging from his pocket on a delicate gold chain. He studies my photograph of the warthog intently through his bifocals and expresses horror at the notion of such an animal as a pet. He doesn't mince his words, but he takes the patient without further ado.

I think that he is happy for the work as all elective surgery has been cancelled in the pandemic. Bringing patients into the hospital unnecessarily exposes the patients and the staff to each other and the hospital is keeping beds open for the coming tide. I am wondering how doctors are keeping afloat financially.

The next time I speak to him I have a young man who shot himself through the hand while cleaning his firearm. He was worried that the pandemic might cause an increase in crime and he may be correct. He is brought into casualty screaming and crying, clutching his left hand to his chest.

'My hand! My hand!'

'Let's have a look.' Blue gloves snap on and I prise his hand away from his body. He has a perfect hole in the centre of his palm, front and back. X-rays show no fracture. All the ligaments and tendons are intact. I call the orthopod.

'I have this guy who shot himself in the hand. Through and through, no bony injury, all movement intact. But I think we should admit him for a washout in the theatre and intravenous antibiotics. What do you think?'

There is a moment's pause and he replies, 'He's an idiot, is what I think.'

I have to smile. He has a great sense of humour.

Seven

I am at my post on a rainy Sunday morning. It is the third day of lockdown and no numbers of new infections are available yet. I was stopped in my first roadblock this morning and they didn't even want to see my paperwork. They just waved me through. Perhaps I have a doomed look about me.

At least I was spared from touching anybody.

I scroll through the updates and see I have received an instruction from the Department of Health as to how we should deal with human remains in the pandemic. No post-mortems will be conducted. Relatives are not allowed to view the deceased. Remains must be double-wrapped and stored in isolation. I read it gloomily. There is also an article telling us that the 10 per cent survival rate on a ventilator is not correct and that it is more like zero. It seems that, in some cases, the virus destroys the lungs completely. For these people there is no hope of recovery.

The bell rings to summon us to a resuscitation in the dialysis unit. I am happy to leave the ED as there is someone coughing like a horse in bed one. It sounds like he has the 'Cora Cora', as the nurses are calling it. Maybe my colleague will see him while I am away at the resuscitation. The less exposure, the better, I think.

I scoot along the corridor and down the stairs. We walk fast but never run as this would engender unnecessary panic. We must always keep up the illusion of unflappability.

When we arrive in the dialysis unit, I see shadows moving

behind a temporary barrier. I pull back the curtain and see the nephrologist holding an oxygen mask on the face of a middle-aged man.

'You rang?' I ask, teasing her with an imitation of Lurch from The Addams Family. 'What's up?'

She looks stressed. 'My patient is having an allergic reaction to the dialysis fluid.'

I put my stethoscope on his chest. Lots of wheezing and he is not moving much air.

'Let's get a nebuliser going and also draw up adrenaline.'

'Oh no,' the nephrologist says. 'I don't think we should give adrenaline. He has high blood pressure and heart disease.'

I look at the monitor, which is chiming and flashing. His blood pressure is low, which is a cardinal sign of a serious allergic reaction. This patient is in trouble.

'We need to give him adrenaline.' I repeat.

'I really don't think we should,' the nephrologist asserts.

'Look,' I want to say. 'You pushed the buzzer to call for my help. I appeared here like a genie. This is what I do every day. If you don't want to take my advice, why did you call me?'

No 'out-loud' voice, I think.

Instead I say, softly so that the patient does not hear, 'If we don't give him adrenaline, he is going to die.'

This seems to convince her.

I inject half an ampule of adrenaline into the muscle of his thigh. It works like magic and within a minute he is breathing easier. We move him onto an ICU bed and cart him away.

The crisis is averted but I have no idea how they are going to dialyse him in the future if he is allergic to the fluid. I will leave that to the nephrologist.

While I am making my way back to the ED, a colleague who is a general surgeon calls me on my mobile. His wife has fallen while running and he thinks that she may have fractured her pelvis. She has blood in her urine. Send her in, I say. I don't remind him that she is not allowed to go jogging during the lockdown. Maybe she has a treadmill at home. All the gyms are closed. I call down to radiology to tell them to expect the patient. The radiologist usually goes at lunchtime and I don't want to have to call her back. We may need a sonar or a CT and, unlike a plain X-ray film, these investigations must be reported by the radiologist. It is often a struggle to get them to agree to come back in to do them, so I find it easier to catch them before they go.

My colleague's wife saunters into the ED 20 minutes later. I have never seen a person with a pelvic fracture walking around. I get her to lie down and examine her. She has no pain in her pelvis. She tells me she slipped on the wet pavement and fell. She finished the run and felt a bit stiff in her hips, but then she noticed blood in her urine.

'Did you eat beetroot recently?' I ask.

She thinks for a moment. 'Actually, I had beetroot chips yesterday.' I present her with a bottle and ask her for a urine sample. I test it and it is completely clear. No blood at all. 'It's the beetroot,' I tell her. I call my colleague and ask him if he still wants me to send her for imaging.

'You decide,' he replies. 'What would you do if she weren't my wife?'

'I would send her home.'

'Send her home then. You know what happens when you try to treat a patient as a special VIP? You get a special screw up.'

Wise words indeed.

Eight

I s it possible that we are becoming used to the pandemic? Jaded even, facing the same chaos day after day? One thing is for sure, it has pulled our ED together like never before. We are looking out for each other, working as a team because we have to. There is no place for ego in times like these.

There is still a queue, but the numbers are definitely down. It seems that people are heeding the call to stay home unless absolutely necessary.

It is most certainly the calm before the storm.

I am sitting at the desk when the red phone rings. The phone is squat and featureless and the colour of a post box. It is for incoming calls only; it has no buttons on its plain countenance and you can't transfer calls.

Once you answer the red phone, whatever is on the other side becomes your problem.

It is linked to the pre-hospital care network so that paramedics and emergency service workers can make a call from their vehicle radio to our landline. Mostly they use it to alert us to their pending arrival with a priority one or unstable patient. This allows the team to get organised and allocate roles, helping to diminish the chaos that surrounds resuscitation. Sometimes they call for advice if they are not coping with a patient on the road.

Over the past few days, the paramedics have called a few times to alert us to a possible Covid-19 case, but they have all been asthma or bronchitis. So far, so good, but I don't expect our luck to hold.

The radio signal, different accents and background noise make it exceedingly difficult to have a conversation on the red phone, so I avoid answering it if I can. But today there is no one else at the nurses' station when the red phone rings. It has a shrill tone and occupies pride of place among the lowly black and grey phones. It is streamlined and shiny. I cannot ignore it.

'Emergency Department, hello?'

The crackle of radio static clips the sentences, but I gather that an emergency crew is at a factory where the staff were cleaning some kind of rolling machine and it was accidentally switched on. The giant rollers turned and drew the hand and arm of a cleaner between them, luckily severing the arm at the elbow rather than sucking the whole person into the machine. The paramedics have applied pressure to slow the bleeding and put up a drip.

'There is no plastic surgeon working at this hospital,' I tell them. 'I think that you should take the patient straight to the Milpark hospital trauma unit unless they are unstable, and we are closer.'

The paramedic reads out the patient's vital signs. Blood pressure on the high side of normal and blood loss less than a cup volume on the scene. Milpark is five minutes further from them and the patient is stable, so I tell them to take the patient to the appropriate facility. We end the conversation.

Thirty minutes later the ambulance bay doorbell rings. Out of the ambulance comes a stretcher. In the middle of the stretcher, wrapped in a linen saver and secured with the belts, is the arm. I am surprised to see it on two counts. Firstly, the cleaner has been taken to Milpark hospital and I'm not sure why the arm is travelling independently. Secondly, it is a young lady's arm with pink nail varnish. On the phone I had not asked the patient's gender and I had assumed an older man.

This crew had been delayed as they had needed a technician to come out and disassemble the machine in order to get the arm out. The other crew with the patient had gone ahead. I explain the misunderstanding. They look confused but go ahead and unclip the cross-straps and move the arm across to our bed. Now I look confused.

'The patient is at Milpark. You must take the arm there; they are waiting for it.' Looking at how badly crushed the end of the arm is, I doubt that a re-implant would be successful, but they will certainly try.

'Oh no, we are a basic ambulance crew,' they say. 'We are not allowed to do inter-hospital transfers. That needs intermediate life support training. You will have to call the base and request a transfer crew.'

This seems ridiculous but the basic ambulance crew is clearly not negotiable, and they are folding their equipment away. I find the nursing unit manager. It is, indeed, true that the basic ambulance crew cannot take the arm. I cannot take it myself in my car as I am the only doctor on duty and can't leave the premises. I suggest that I send it in an Uber taxi but that is apparently against hospital policy.

Time is of the essence with re-implantation so I call the ambulance dispatch control room and tell them that I need an urgent transfer to Milpark. They ask if the patient is stable. I look over at the lightly freckled, pale forearm packed in wet saline. 'Yes. Um. Stable.' I don't want to use 'he' or 'she' as that would seem dishonest, and I can't say 'it'. Stable means the condition is not about to change, which is true of the arm. You could also, technically, call a dead person stable.

They will have to figure it out when they get here.

Nine

For the first time in many years, I feel fearful at work. As a young doctor in the ED I used to worry that a patient would come in with something that I could not manage and that I would be out of my depth.

Nobody wants to see a doctor who doesn't know what they are doing. And no one knows what they are doing all of the time. In fact, when I was first qualified, I didn't know what I was doing most of the time. When I think back, I shudder to think how much I missed and how many people I may have actively harmed. But, as any inveterate liar knows, the most convincing lies are those that you persuade yourself are true. After years of fooling yourself and others, you come to believe your own untruths.

You also don't know enough to know what you don't know. Those middle years are the most dangerous.

I think that there are few things as frightening as being in charge of something that is spinning out of control. The intense fear when you realise that you don't know what you are doing; that the situation is heading for a crash and you feel helpless to change the course of events. That horrible moment when you know that you are alone with an unstable patient, that you are their last hope, and you don't have the knowledge or the equipment to help them.

As time passed, I became more confident. Now I am the one that younger colleagues call to help them in a crisis. A junior doctor told me that she sighed with relief when she saw my car in the parking lot because she knew that she was not alone. It is a compliment that other doctors feel happy to share a shift with me and I am glad that I don't panic every time the ED doorbell rings.

Maybe a small quiver of anxiety, every now and then, but nothing like it used to be.

Now I am fearful again.

Fear likes to be in the dark and it is powerful when concealed. I wake up uneasy and lie quietly in the half light of dawn, trying to unpack my worries. I lead them out, one by one, into the daylight of my rational mind.

I am afraid because, from the inside, I know that our healthcare system cannot cope with the coming months. I don't want to have to be the one to decide on who to ventilate and who to leave. I am afraid of running out of resources and beds and having to turn people away.

Yes, I am afraid for myself, but I am more afraid for my loved ones. Afraid that they will not be able to get help without me as their advocate. I fear being the vector of the virus because it feels like I know better than they do how dreadful this monster will be when let loose upon the vulnerable. And we are all vulnerable. Does the virus have a 'type'? If so, am I its type?

The medical profession is getting to know a new demon and trying to look it in the eye without showing fear. I am trying to look it in the eye and stay more than a metre away.

We are all rushing around, trying to predict the shifting landscape in a sandstorm and set up contingency plans based on what other countries can teach us. In a year this will all be over, I suppose, one way or another.

I am afraid of the failure of both myself and the system in which I have worked for almost 30 years. I am afraid for my snoopies and my family if I am culled as their guardian and provider.

With a sigh, I pull myself out of bed and into the shower. I make the water as hot as possible as I hear the virus doesn't like the heat. I also hear it likes people with type-A blood group.

That's me.

I touch the screen of my mobile, bringing it to life, checking the time and facing the day.

Today I am working with François, a smiley doctor from Democratic Republic of the Congo. He has a charming French accent, shiny shoes and expensive aftershave. He has a few gaps in his knowledge but overall, the patients like him. I have noticed that the sisters tend to bypass him and come to me with the more urgent patients. This can be annoying, especially when it is busy, and I am balancing nine patients and he is buffing his nails. Sometimes I must prevent myself from pointing out that there are actually two doctors working in the unit.

A middle-aged man comes in complaining of chest pain. Chest pain is always triaged as a priority, so he comes straight through to a bed in the resus area. The sister does an ECG and walks right past François in order to bring it to me. I am busy with another patient but, after one glance at the ECG, I excuse myself from the consultation.

Passing my desk for a fresh piece of notepaper, I present myself at the foot of the bed and start to gather information on the chest pain. When did it start, what were you doing, how severe is it, what is your history, what is your family history?

Although he is only 50 years old, he has all the risk factors. He smokes and has high blood pressure, and his father died from a heart attack. He is very overweight and has high cholesterol.

I move from the foot of the bed to examine him. He is sweating profusely and his colour is not good. I explain to him that I think that he is having a heart attack. His pain is typical, he has risk factors and his ECG is abnormal. He takes the news calmly and chews up the aspirin that I give him. I can see that he still has severe pain, but his blood pressure is too low for me to give him morphine. In addition, the ECG suggests that the heart attack is affecting the right side of his heart, which means I cannot give medication that drops the blood pressure. With right-sided damage, the heart relies on the blood returning from the rest of the body in order to keep pumping.

He asks me to call his wife. She sounds distracted and goes off on a tangent about his unhealthy lifestyle and ongoing problems with heartburn. I don't want to tell her on the telephone that he is having a heart attack as she might panic and have an accident driving to the hospital. She says it is a bad time as they are in lockdown and her husband was supposed to go to the grocery store. I want to tell her that this threat is more immediate and life-threatening than coronavirus, but I would rather speak to her in person.

When she arrives, she spends five minutes berating the poor man about his shocking lifestyle and diet. She is anorexically thin and dressed up to the nines with perfectly coiffed hair and layers of makeup. I interject and tell her that he is having a heart attack. She stares at me, a completely vacant look on her face.

'Heart attack? No, no. It's just reflux.'

'Um, no, actually it's a heart attack.'

'Just tell him it's reflux,' she says in a stage whisper.

'I can't do that. He knows that he is having a heart attack. He needs to understand what's happening and sign consent for an angiogram.'

She chews gum and stares at me. Sweat rolls down her husband's face. 'So, what is actually wrong with him?'

'He is having a heart attack.' I say it slightly louder. Maybe my voice is muffled from the mask, but her face is still completely blank. 'The heart is a muscle supplied by vessels, like a highway running to a suburb.' I turn the file over and draw a heart on the back, complete with blood supply. 'One of the vessels is narrowed, like road works on the highway, and then a clot gets stuck there – like a car breaking down in the one open lane.' I draw the blockage.

'Now the blood supply cannot reach the area supplied by the highway and that part of the heart muscle runs out of oxygen and dies. That area of dead heart muscle is called a heart attack and the outcome varies, depending on where the blockage is and how big the area of dead muscle is.' I draw an area of dead muscle on the heart. 'From the ECG, I think that his blockage is in the right coronary artery.' I draw a crude rendition of the right coronary artery. 'The cardiologist is on his way in and he will do an angiogram. That means that he will thread a catheter through an artery in the groin, all the way to the heart, and put in dye to see where the blockage is. Then, if possible, he will open the blocked vessel and put a little supporting pipe inside to hold it open. That's called a stent.'

More sweat rolls down the man's face. I am worried about his blood pressure and I call the cardiologist to see how far the catheterisation team is. They are en route and he tells me to take the patient to ICU in the meantime. I tell him that the blood pressure is low. He knows me well enough to hear the concern in my voice. We run through the medication that I have given so far. Aspirin, intravenous paracetamol for pain, enoxaparin and clopidogrel to thin the blood. An oral dose of a cholesterol-lowering agent. I have held back on the nitrates and morphine because of the blood pressure. We agree that the ECG shows a right-sided heart attack. He tells me that we are good to go to the ICU. He has booked the bed.

The temptation is to tell the sister to take the patient up to ICU and let me go back to my interrupted consultation. But Grim is around; I can feel him. The patient is still sweating profusely and is restless in the bed, shifting around and taking deep breaths. I decide to go up to ICU with him and stay there until the cardiologist or the anaesthetist arrives.

As I move him over onto the ICU bed, he arrests. It almost looks like he is holding his breath or having a seizure. His face turns bright red, his teeth clamp together, and he starts to grunt. The monitor goes crazy.

'Give me the defibrillator!' I call out to the sister who is helping me. She looks at me, confused. The defibrillator shocks the heart, in the hope that it will restart again in a correct rhythm.

'The defib! Quick!'

She nudges the defib trolley closer and I push the charge button. Gel, paddles, clear, shock. I immediately start CPR. He opens his eyes and asks, 'Hey doc. How's my heart?' I want to collapse against the wall and say, 'Your heart? Dude, what about my heart?'

I stand guard next to the bed until the cardiologist arrives. He looks amazed that so much has happened in the 20 minutes since we spoke. He gets busy with his echo machine, looking at the heart through a sonar probe, and I excuse myself. He has my mobile number if he needs me and the patient; I was busy with must be wondering what is going on.

Outside the ICU I find the wife, tottering around in her heels and looking vague. I give her an update, telling her that the cardiologist is with him now and they should be in the catheterisation lab within 10 minutes. I tell her that he is still critical and that his heart had stopped briefly but we had managed to get it started again. My clear-cut save from Grim is pretty impressive, even to me, but my heroism is lost on her. She looks at me blankly, chewing gum and fiddling with her hair.

'So... what's actually wrong with him?'

I stare at her incredulously. 'He's having a heart attack.'

She looks bored and slightly irritated. 'Is he still having a heart attack?'

'Yes,' I reply, taking a deep breath and glancing towards the heavens for help. 'He's still having it. He will be having a heart attack until we open the vessel.'

God help me, I think, and scuttle back to the ED.

Ten

I am feeling slightly more optimistic today. At the helm of the pulmonologists in Gauteng is one of the most capable doctors I know and, even though he admits that we are flying by the seat of our pants, I have faith in him. The pulmonologists, as a group, are going to be the epicentre of the storm and it is good to know that South Africa has retained such intellect and experience. I see on the WhatsApp group today that they have managed to keep five patients with severe coronavirus disease alive without ventilating them in our Gauteng region.

On the downside, the hospital groups have figured out that we are going to run short of personal protective equipment and are now telling us to sterilise our masks in the oven at home and re-use them the next day.

I am reminded of the years when I had just qualified, when the terror of HIV hit home. We all wore goggles and double gloves and every drop of blood was regarded as pure poison.

The risk of contracting HIV now pales into insignificance in the face of coronavirus. HIV is far less contagious, has much slower progression and there is, at least, treatment available.

I feel nostalgic for the old days. The surgical intake ward at Chris Hani Baragwanath Hospital was affectionately known as 'The Pit'. The Pit smelled like blood, alcohol and vomit and was strewn with ghastly injuries. There were benches full of people waiting and a scarred table where wide-eyed students and junior doctors huddled, facing an endless tableau of the dead and dying.

Triage consisted of a long-suffering medical officer on a chair at the door. He – I never saw a woman in that role – would place a red sticker on the forehead of the patients that he deemed about to die, and the porter would push them to the front of the queue. The wheelchairs and stretchers were hosed off outside the entrance. There was no security check – people walked, staggered or were carried in straight off the street.

When I was a student, I saw the professor of surgery in The Pit. It was a Saturday night in Soweto and the trauma patients streamed through the door. A woman in surgical scrubs appeared for a magical moment and disappeared just as quickly. She was small in stature but big in presence, with highlighted blonde hair peeking out beneath her theatre cap and quick blue eyes. She was wearing heavy gold jewelry and a theatre gown. I felt like I had seen a shiny unicorn passing through a matt version of Dante's Inferno. For years, I wondered whether she had been a figment of my fevered imagination.

Years later, in private practice, I became her surgical assistant. I had been working with her for more than a year when I saw her in the queue at the local supermarket.

'Hi.' I said. In the awkward silence that followed I realised that she did not recognise me. In the theatre we were shrouded in hats and masks.

'I'm your assistant.'

'Oh!' She was clearly relieved. 'I didn't recognise you with your clothes on.' The look on the other customers' faces was priceless and we both burst out laughing. From that day on, we became friends as well as colleagues.

She had come into private practice late in her life, having been the head of surgery at Baragwanath Hospital for years. In those days gender discrimination was still flourishing in fields like general surgery. The professor was a dedicated surgeon and a ferocious fighter for equal rights. I assisted her for 10 years; we operated three times a week, starting at three in the afternoon and working late into the night.

A pharmaceutical rep who used to know her while she worked at Baragwanath heard that I was assisting her.

'I heard a story about her, but I don't know if it's true.'

'Tell me.'

'She used to do these hectic long cases. They could go on for 10 hours or more. She had the houseman helping her, holding the liver retractor, for the whole day. The houseman was post-call, probably hypoglycaemic, and eventually he fainted. Because he was standing behind her, the prof didn't notice. Everyone in the theatre was terrified to speak but eventually the anaesthetist piped up.

'Prof, excuse me, but I think your houseman has collapsed.'

She looked up and said 'Oh no. Do you have another one?'''

I thought about this story for a hot second before saying 'I'm sure it's true.'

She was a tough task mistress. She demanded complete focus and silence in her theatre. If I shifted my weight from one foot to the other, she would tell me sharply to stand still. If my hand strayed from its dedicated duty, she would rap my knuckles. She took on difficult cases and patients that other surgeons had declined. She was always impeccably turned out and fiercely polite. I learned an enormous amount from her.

She taught me how to put in a chest drain and take out a spleen – although the latter was of dubious value in the ED. She told me that all bleeding stops eventually. The first stage of bleeding begged the question, 'Why did I take this case?' The second, 'Why did I become a surgeon?' and the third was 'Why was I born?'

She would quiz me on the various steps of surgical challenges and fix me with an unwavering gaze if I hesitated. I once made the mistake of pointing out a small bleeding vessel that would not have been visible from her side of the patient. She stopped operating immediately and placed her instruments deliberately on the draped tray. The silence in the theatre was deafening.

'Doctor,' she addressed me formally, 'I do know what a red blood cell looks like. However, if you doubt my competence, please do feel free to take over the surgery.'

I felt a flush creep up my neck and mumbled 'sorry' into my mask. The anaesthetist sniggered. I waited outside for her to change out of her scrubs and into her twin set and pearls.

I took a deep breath. 'As your assistant, it is my job to help you. I wasn't criticising you or meaning to insult you. I was trying to help, and if you take issue with that, I won't say anything and you'll be the one to come back at three in the morning to re-open.'

She stared at me for a moment and replied 'You are quite correct. I am deeply sorry that I spoke to you in that fashion. I shall not do it again.'

She was true to her word. We worked side by side, long into more dark nights than I care to remember. She called me her 'secret weapon' and, on one occasion, suggested that we 'bottle my blood'.

When she broke her ankle on an early morning walk, she operated all day before having her own surgery in the evening. I asked her why she didn't cancel her list and she told me that her patients needed their operations.

Her recovery period saw me double up as her assistant and driver. She would point her crutch at things she needed and bang it on the ground if I was not quick enough to respond. Sometimes I didn't know whether to laugh or cry.

On the ward rounds we tried desperately not to laugh out loud at her formal manner and we lived in secret fear of her sharp tongue. Beneath her constructed self, she was thoughtful and kind and genuinely wanted to teach.

I think of her today as I read the pulmonologists' and intensive care specialists' posts on the groups. I have so much respect for their dedication and commitment. Perhaps, with leaders like this, we have a chance.

Eleven

In the early hours I hear the rain roaring on the tin roof. Dawn pulls me from sleep with the faint boom of thunder, like waves on a distant reef. It is Monday, day four of the lockdown. The confirmed positives were around 1200 last night with a second death confirmed and my optimism has evaporated.

Early morning rain is unusual on the Highveld – the day usually starts with clear blue skies and builds towards purple afternoon thunderstorms.

As the sun rises the world is cloaked in a million jewels. Tiny sparkles hang on every leaf and blade of grass and the terraced lawns shimmer silver over green. The greyhounds bound along, diamonds flying up in their wake and their tracks black on the wet grass.

They only get one walk today because I am working the 10 am to 10 pm shift.

It's a long day and the ED is absurdly busy. I am alone because it turns out that the charming French François is not a medical doctor after all. A few weeks ago, a patient had a bad experience with him and complained to the Medical Council. We received a letter with the dreaded Health Professions Council of South Africa logo last week and, on further investigation, found that François had fraudulently assumed the identity of a long-retired general practitioner.

His name disappeared off the ED roster with immediate effect and, without him, I am hopelessly outnumbered.

A few days ago, we opened a parallel room where all respiratory cases are seen. The doctors take turns in the 'regular' ED and the 'Covid' side, trying to limit cross-contamination. Today I must run between the two, because of François. I can't believe he fooled us all and I scan the packed waiting room with despair. Where do all these people come from?

It seems like everyone in South Africa has a sore throat and a cough and this is their preferred ED. Amid the chaos, the paramedics bring an unstable patient. Impolitely, they do not call on the red phone to alert us to their pending arrival. Even more impolitely, they have totally missed what is really going on with the patient and tell me that he is the victim of a low-impact car accident.

He had just departed from his home, driving along the road in which he lives, and he veered off the road at a low speed and collided with a parked car. The fact that the patient was barely conscious and has no recordable blood pressure seems to have escaped them entirely. The possibility that he crashed his car because he lost consciousness and not the opposite has not been entertained.

The two paramedics are fresh-faced and eager, and I don't want to damage our relationship by showing my annoyance. Also, the day that I break my reputation for being the coolest cat in the hospital, it will be over something much more momentous than a young colleague's inexperience.

The patient is massively overweight, and I move anxiously around the bed trying to figure out what is wrong with him. He has a rapid, thready pulse and is cold and sweaty. I ask the sisters to put up a drip and do an ECG. As I am examining his distended white belly, I see the cardiac monitor change from a regular rhythm into a squiggly wave and I check his pulse. Nothing.

'Start CPR!' I shout. I get up onto the bed and start compressing his chest.

'Bring the defib!' The resus room erupts into chaos. Sisters bring drugs and a ventilation bag. I do one cycle of CPR then check the rhythm with the paddles. The heart is fibrillating – quivering and not beating, which is what hearts do when they are dying. If you are early enough, and lucky enough, you can shock it and it will start again. I hit the charge buttons and the machine whines as it builds up joules.

'Clear!'

Everyone steps back and I press the shock button. The huge man jolts on the bed. I smell singeing chest hair and realise that I forgot to put gel on the paddles. I start CPR again. The door to the resus room swings open and the surgeon barges in. He is a bull of a man with a mane of dark, wavy hair and a labile temperament.

'My neighbour came in after a motor accident. Where is he?'

'The accident is the least of his problems,' I answer as I rock back off the bed and let the sister give two breaths with the bag and mask that she is holding ready over his nose and mouth. 'He arrested a minute after he got here.'

'Arrested?' He stares at me in disbelief. I wonder if he knows that this patient is his neighbour. I suppose he looks quite different, laid out naked on his back with equipment snaking over him.

I address the sister. 'One minute to rhythm check and change.'

Back to the surgeon. 'Yep. Arrested. Could you try and get some history from his family?'

After a few moments on his mobile phone, he tells me that the patient had back pain yesterday and went to another local hospital where he was diagnosed with a urinary tract infection. He had blood in his urine. He got a script for an antibiotic but only started it just before he left home this morning. The surgeon is shouting simultaneously at the family and at the ED receptionist who is trying to open the file.

Could this be a severe allergic reaction? The patient doesn't have any swelling of his face or airway, but an allergy could account for his non-existent blood pressure and arrest.

'He's had a heart attack!' The surgeon announces with authority.

He speed-dials the cardiologist, who is also in the hospital. Soon there are two of them watching me do CPR.

'I don't think this is a heart attack,' I grunt as I push hard and fast on the centre of his chest. 'By the time he lost consciousness and blood pressure from a heart attack, he would have already arrested. He had a pulse when he got here. I think he has a ruptured aortic aneurysm.'

'Oh no,' the surgeon argues. 'He doesn't have an aneurysm.'

'How do you know?'

'He is my neighbour.' A simple, emphatic reply. I raise my eyebrows at this logic. How would he know the state of his neighbour's aorta?

The next rhythm check tells me we have a pulse. I get off the bed and call the radiologist. I need a super-urgent sonar of his abdomen. The cardiologist and surgeon take hold of the foot of the stretcher. They are planning to take him immediately to the cardiac catheterisation laboratory to address the heart attack. I take hold of the head of the bed. I am planning a sonar of his abdomen before he goes anywhere. They tug. I tug. The sister brings a printed ECG and it is abnormal. They wave it in triumph. I shake my head.

'The ECG will be abnormal after 5 minutes of CPR and a shock. We must wait for the ultrasound.'

The radiologist arrives with her sonar machine and they agree to wait a few moments. When the sonar confirms free fluid in the abdomen due to a ruptured aortic aneurysm, I resist the impulse to fist-pump the air.

The diagnosis is made. But now we must fix it. It is not ideal for the surgeon to operate on his friend but there is no other option. We dash along the corridor to the theatre. There is no anaesthetist so I stay with the patient as I can't leave him unattended in the corridor. I need to keep an eye on his pulse. It is racing due to the adrenalin that we gave him.

The surgeon has changed into scrubs and has a paper theatre hat perched on top of his luxurious hair. 'His blood pressure is too high!' He shouts at me. I stare at him. In the ED we have various tricks to bring the blood pressure up. But in a case like this, I have no idea of how to bring it down. I miss the greyhounds. I miss the sea. I briefly close my eyes and imagine walking the snoopies on the beach. I can see them running on the sand, chasing the frothy apron of surf. I can feel the tug of the breeze and the harsh call of the seagulls. But the clanging is not a seagull, it is the noise of the monitor.

'Get platelets and blood! Get his blood pressure down! He's moving on the table, for Christ's sake! Must I put my knee on his chest?' The surgeon is in a spin. 'Suck, suck!' I don't know who he is instructing as there is no assistant. I am trying to keep the patient sedated and I can't operate the suction anyway as I am not sterile.

'Oh my God, there's so much blood!'

I would imagine that a surgeon would be accustomed to the sight of blood. I get my mobile phone out of the little pouch around my waist and start trying to find an anaesthetist. I need to get back to the ED as there is no other doctor on duty. I don't know how to operate the anaesthetic machine and this patient is too unstable for me to dope. The last anaesthetic I gave was in medical school. I scroll through my list of contacts on my phone, thinking who has a theatre list and might be in the hospital.

After a few calls I find someone to take over from me and I wish them all luck as I leave.

Back in the ED, I take two minutes to sip some tepid tea and jot a few notes. I have a medical student doing her elective with me and her eyes are wide. She is originally from Ghana and her accent is difficult to understand.

'You don't see much rabies here?' she asks.

'No,' I reply, distracted by the notes I am writing about the aneurism. 'Do you see a lot in Ghana?'

'Oh yes,' she nods earnestly. 'A whole ward, full!'

I stop writing and look up. 'You have a whole ward just for rabies?'

'Yes, yes.' She is very sincere.

I frown. 'Is there no vaccination programme?'

She looked confused. 'No. People don't want vaccinations.'

'It shouldn't be up to the general public. It's preventable, so the government should just enforce it.' I am back to writing while I speak, but her silence gives me pause. I look up to find her staring at me as if I am Hitler reincarnated. I think back on our conversation and I realise that she was saying babies, not rabies.

The misunderstanding is resolved, and the medical student goes to make tea, passing a grey-haired lady who is hovering anxiously in the hallway.

'My husband is having chest pain.'

Not another one, I think.

'One of the sisters at reception will triage him and do an ECG,' I tell her.

'There is no one at reception.'

The clock above her head tells me it is just past seven. Nursing and reception staff are thin on the ground because of shift change. Some leave early, some are late, and most are busy in the hand-over process. They are signing drug registers and giving patient details to the new shift. I get up and follow the lady out.

There, in a totally deserted waiting room, her husband is sitting in the wheelchair where she left him. His head is lolling to the side; he is grey and not breathing.

'Oh no!' I leap forward and grab the wheelchair. Taking off with speed, I charge through the doors and into the resus area, shouting for the sisters as I go. I jam on brakes at the first bed and attempt to transfer the man from the wheelchair onto the bed. This is a logistical impossibility. He is about double my weight and size and he is, literally, a dead weight. I tilt his torso forward, grab his belt and kick the wheelchair away. Now he is face down on the pillow with his upper body half on the bed and I am holding him by the back of the belt with my right hand and trying to lift his legs with my left. He is too heavy.

'Help!' I shout, feeling ridiculous.

'He's not breathing,' his wife informs me anxiously.

I bite back a sarcastic comment. Working in the ED encourages a black sense of humour which can be an effective defense against all the sadness in the world. Tragedy has a way of raining down in a blinding torrent and sometimes I must remind myself that being kind also counts as active intervention.

This guy needs CPR before kindness, though, and we start our well-practised dance. The sisters arrive with the medical student and they help me get him on the bed. CPR is inherently unkind and our attempt to restart the heart can be brutal – breaking ribs and electrocuting the patient as we go. My wrists ache and my eyes are burning with fatigue, but I start pressing on his chest to the mechanised metronome in my head. It is my third resuscitation of the day and I am exhausted. I feel spat out and spent, but I manage to pull him away from Grim.

He walks out of the hospital four days later.

Twelve

I
t is day eight of the lockdown and there are seven confirmed deaths. I have ordered a reusable mask with filters that can be washed.

I hear that there are at least two subtypes of the virus and one seems to be much more lethal than the other. Protocols are popping up like mushrooms and I am given two little tablets this morning when I arrive at work. They are hydroxychloroquine – a medication to prevent malaria – and it seems that it might help to prevent us getting coronavirus. I am not sure about them, so I put them in my pocket. I will think about whether to take them or not when I have a quiet moment. They have quite a few side effects and I need to read up on their efficacy.

I hear that a colleague, a general practitioner, is on a ventilator at a nearby hospital. The pulmonologist looking after her shows me her X-rays and the outlook is grim. The difference in the X-ray from yesterday to today is truly frightening. Patches have appeared overnight like a rampant overgrowth, consolidation spreading like a white wildfire across the previously dark lung fields.

This is the first of many such X-rays and patients in distress, I am sure; water is beginning to trickle through the seams of the dyke and I can feel the pressure of the wall of ocean, as yet unseen, mounting on the other side.

We are distracted from this worrying discussion by a woman running into the ED with an unresponsive child in her arms. The child is a nasty shade of blue and the sister in triage takes them straight through to the resuscitation room. The child is gasping, and we start CPR. Mom tells us that her daughter choked on a piece of cheese. Her husband did back slaps and the Heimlich manoeuvere, but the child is barely breathing.

I listen to her chest and she is wheezing on both sides. If an inhaled foreign body is stuck in the upper airway there will be stridor – a high-pitched wheezing – and harsh noises from the throat area with each attempted breath. If the foreign body is sucked in deeper than the larynx it can go down one main bronchus – usually the right one because it is straighter– and the wheezing will be on one side only.

I nebulise the child with a bronchodilator, adrenaline and cortisone. Her colour improves a bit and I make a call to the nearest paediatric ICU to transfer her. They accept her and I get busy arranging a portable chest X-ray and an advanced life support ambulance to take her across.

We are all set to go when the sister, an elderly lady with many years of mileage in the ED, shakes her head.

'This baby is not right.'

I reassess the little girl. She is sitting up on her own now, but each breath is an enormous effort. She is using her arms and body to help inflate her lungs; her face is slightly swollen and hundreds of tiny bleeds have appeared around her eyes from the effort of breathing.

'You are right.' I say to the sister. I don't think that she is going to make the 10-minute journey to the ICU. We are going to need to intubate and ventilate her.

The parents watch me with big eyes as I explain that I need to sedate her and breathe for her as I am concerned that she will get tired and lose her airway en route.

I write up the drugs for the sedation and call the accepting doctor at the paediatric ICU while the sisters get things ready.

'Are you sure it's not coronavirus?' he asks.

'I don't think so,' I answer. 'Very sudden onset and a typical history of choking.' I just can't explain why she is so short of breath and wheezing both sides.

He agrees that I should intubate the child if she is unstable, even though it means that her transfer will be delayed. We will need to wait for a different ambulance with a paediatric ventilator.

The intubation goes as smoothly as can be expected and the little girl is transported by helicopter in a relatively stable condition.

It is a hectic progression of illness and has me scratching my head as to what, exactly, is wrong with her. I call the accepting ICU and leave five messages before one of the paediatricians calls me back. She tells me that they still have no idea of what the root cause of the bronchospasm is. The little girl stopped breathing a few hours after her arrival at the ICU and had to be put on ECMO, which stands for extracorporeal membrane oxygenation. It is like a lung bypass for very severe pneumonia and poor oxygenation. She is also on dialysis because her kidneys failed from the poor oxygen supply and subsequent acidosis.

A very scary case for the ED but much scarier for the parents, of course, who watched as we wrestled Grim for the upper hand. It was a close call and I am sure they will spend the rest of her life terrified that it will happen again.

No more cheese for her, I think to myself.

In all the excitement I forgot the chloroquine tablets in the pocket of my scrubs, and they didn't make it through the wash. Two little bits of melted plastic are all that remains of the capsules.

I suppose I will have to ask management for some more. I doubt that they will give me any.

Thirteen

The rain pours down all night as we enter the ninth day of lockdown. I hear that the ED at St Augustine's Hospital in Durban has closed because of deaths from coronavirus. The entire staff was exposed to three positive patients over the past few weeks. The patients passed away yesterday and now the whole staff is quarantined. I leave home in the half-light, the mist thick and the roads awash in water.

I feel like I should go back to the bible and read that passage about Noah and the flood. Maybe there is a message in there for us.

When I arrive in the ED I am met by a frightened team. They had their first death from possible coronavirus last night. A 40-year-old previously well woman came in with shortness of breath and died shortly after arrival. It seems that seven members of the team, including two doctors, were exposed. They have been sent home, awaiting the patient's swab result.

The hospital is a gracious old lady with wide corridors and gleaming floors. Outside the cool glass, the suburbs of Johannesburg are a hazy green canopy. The rain is lifting but the world is still misty.

I recall a different hospital with a similar view in a much poorer area of town. It was one of my first shifts as a final year medical student. A pale young woman was brought into the ED in a wheelchair. She was slumped sideways, moaning and clutching her stomach. Vomit streaked the corners of her mouth and her hair stood directly upwards as if she had been pulled out of a thicket by her feet. I found myself staring at her in fascination. It was like every strand of hair had the capacity to defy gravity.

As a sixth year student, I saw the patients first and then presented my findings to the Intern. The Intern would then assess the patient and either manage them in the ED or refer them to the registrar. The registrar is a doctor who is doing five years of specialist training.

Within this system, then, there are junior registrars, who have just joined the circuit, and senior registrars, who are almost finished training. Once specialised, they either leave the government service and go into private practice, or they stay on as a consultant. Most consultants make sure their registrars are well practised in all possible emergencies before leaving them alone in the unit. In theory, the consultant is also on call for the 24 hours that his or her unit is on intake, but it is very rare to find a consultant actually present in the hospital after hours.

On that day neither the intern nor the registrar was in the unit. I went ahead and saw the patient.

First, I circled the bed to check on her hair. It was still standing upright like a thousand antennas. I wanted to ask her if she had brushed it upwards repeatedly to achieve this style but decided against that line of questioning. Between groaning and retching she told me that she was 27 years old and had been having severe abdominal pain for the past few hours. She was about 36 weeks pregnant. The monitor over her bed complained about her low blood pressure and high pulse. I fumbled with the sonar probe for a few minutes before concluding that there was something seriously wrong here. I was still an absolute novice with the sonar, but I could not find the uterus and the baby was up under the liver, not in the pelvis where it should be. There was no foetal pulse.

I would have to find the intern or page the gynaecology registrar myself. I knew it would not be politically correct for a sixth-year student to page the registrar. Students spoke to interns. Interns spoke to registrars. Registrars spoke to consultants. That was the chain of command. But I could not find the intern anywhere – she was not answering her pager and I could not find her in the wards or laboratory.

The alarm on the machine was chiming louder. The blood pressure was even lower. I paged the registrar. She sounded annoyed but appeared in the ED a few moments later and commandeered the ultrasound machine. My fears were confirmed – the young mother had ruptured her uterus in labour, and the baby was dead, floating free in the abdomen. A pregnant uterus has a massive blood supply and she had lost a lot of blood from the torn muscles and vessels. It was a life-threatening situation.

There was still no intern, so I signed the consent for emergency surgery with the patient and pushed the bed to the theatre. This would be the third operation that I had attended. The first two had been Caesarian sections with a jaded registrar. I got the impression he had been in the system forever and one of the interns told me that he could not seem to pass his exams. He certainly knew how to operate, though.

I had gazed at the pregnant uterus, unveiled by a few smooth sweeps of the scalpel. It looked like a bald head popping up out of the pelvis, nodding forward, the ovaries like low-slung ears on the sides. That registrar had mumbled into his mask and pushed my hands around, trying to show me how to assist him.

The registrar tonight was incredibly young, her eyes worried and her hands fiddling anxiously with the instruments. She made a few tentative passes with the blade before she got going. As we opened the abdomen a wave of blood welled up to meet us. The suction gurgled greedily but the blood just kept coming. The registrar kept swabbing and sucking. The monitor chimed unhappily. Blood pressure was dangerously low. I could see the anaesthetist moving edgily around on the darkened periphery. I stared into the brightly lit abdomen and stated the obvious.

'She's bleeding too much. Should we do a hysterectomy?'

The registrar shook her head. 'We don't have consent.'

I looked at the suction bottle. Almost two litres. This woman could not afford to lose any more blood. 'It doesn't matter about the consent,' I said. 'It's life-saving. What's the point of trying to save her uterus if she's dead?'

The registrar shook her head again. 'No. She's only 27 and this baby is gone. She will want a family. We can pack the abdomen and wait for the consultant. She isn't bleeding much anymore.'

Under the drapes, big drops of blood were tap tap tapping on the linoleum floor. I stepped back and lifted the heavy green linen to expose the sinister pool. 'She is bleeding past the swabs. We must do a hysterectomy!' My words hung in the air. The registrar's dark eyes met mine over our masks. Softly, she answered, 'I don't know how to do a hysterectomy.'

A simple statement of fact.

I wanted to shout 'What? How can you be the registrar on call and not know how to do a hysterectomy?' I stopped myself, asking what the point of such recrimination would be. She already looked completely stricken.

I certainly didn't have the first idea of how to do a hysterectomy, and those days were long before Google.

I stripped off my gloves and drew a sample of blood for matching at the blood bank. I felt bad taking a compatibility test as she needed every ruby drop, but if we couldn't stop the bleeding then the next best thing would be to get blood to replace it. My theatre gown flying out behind me, I galloped out of the theatre, down the corridor and up the stairs. In full flight, I stepped on the long green tie of my gown and fell. Grunting as I hit the floor, I slid along on my stomach, my arms outstretched, and the precious tube of blood cradled safely in my hands. In front of me, at eye level, I saw the bottom of an office door shutting, a pair of shiny shoes and a briefcase. At 9 pm in a deserted corridor, that could mean one thing only. A consultant!

'Are you a consultant?' I gasped, springing to my feet. He

looked at me sceptically. Wild-eyed and covered in blood, I must have been quite a sight.

'Yes,' his voice was cautious. 'Why?'

'You have to come with me!' Instinctively, I stretched out my arms to bar his escape. He shrank back. 'We have this patient on the table, and she needs a hysterectomy and the registrar doesn't know how to do one and she's bleeding out. The patient! The patient is bleeding out. Not the registrar!' The story tumbled out between gasps.

I clearly recall that he didn't ask one question about my convoluted tale of woe. He just said, 'Come.' We hurried to the theatre, where he did the hysterectomy, carefully showing us the steps so that we would know for the future.

To this day I have no idea who that consultant was. I did not ask his name and I never saw him again. But I will never forget his swift hands and quiet demeanour. I think of him again now as I stare out at the thick autumn afternoon. The rain has lifted, and the air is close and humid.

I suppose that, today, I am that consultant and I am wearing that pair of shoes. People always remark on how calm I seem. This is often discordant with my internal world but perhaps my childhood calling to become an actress has paid off. Now I have a reputation to uphold – I am She Who Never Shouts.

If you pretend anything for long enough, it will eventually become your reality and luckily my professional persona is not too far removed from the way that I am naturally in the world. This persona has been moulded through a combination of patient feedback and occasional introspection. Now I slip in and out of my professional mask without conscious awareness, although I often must remind myself not to use my 'out-loud' voice.

I remind myself that people are not coming to the ED to ask my opinion on their lifestyle choices or parenting styles. People can do really dumb things, which probably seemed like a good idea at the time. They are often afraid and belligerent and can be very difficult. If you want to survive without being assaulted or, even worse, sued, you must learn to keep your mouth shut and your eyes and ears open.

I stare out of the tall window. The wooden frames are thick with years of enamel paint, and the sun paints long, golden rectangles on the floor. The sky is summer blue, and clouds stretch all the way to the horizon, ruler-straight on the bottoms as if resting on a sheet of glass. I see my faint reflection and barely recognise myself. When my auburn curls turned grey, I cut my hair short. The corners of my eyes and mouth are lined. I joke that ED doctors age in dog years – one year for everyone else is seven years for us. I am weary and watchful and sometimes tired, but I am never old.

Time to get my calm self back to work. I trot down the wide staircase and double back to the service entrance of the ED. After 30 years in the same hospital, I am a mouse in a too-familiar maze.

Fourteen

ay 10 and we are almost halfway to the mystical date set for our release from lockdown. I feel like Robinson Crusoe, crossing off the numbers on an island full of masked people. We are together in a kind of isolated daze, drifting past each other with minimal communication. I can feel that the ED team is tired.

Not that the virus will be gone by day 21, any more than it only started on day one. On the Wednesday before the lockdown, the restaurants were still full. People were taking advantage because the lockdown started on Thursday and so the virus was only of relevance from Friday.

Today I arrive at work to the update of 1585 infections and nine deaths but also six deaths allegedly from police brutality inflicted on disobedient citizens. I am disappointed that, some 25 years since the dawn of democracy, some things in South Africa have not changed.

A new day and the score is one to Grim, nil to me. Grim's point was uncontested – an ancient grandfather with a living will, brought in as he breathed his last. My job is really just paperwork, filling in lots of tiny blocks in a grubby carbon copy book. I gather information from his identity book and his dry-eyed family. It had been time for him to go. At ten o'clock, tea is served in a pleasingly hot, heavy teapot. It is set up in the side ward, with a plate of crustless egg sandwiches trapped under cling film.

Since yesterday, a visor from the local hardware store has been added to my armamentarium. I take it off and wash my hands under the hottest water that I can bear before touching the food.

We are trotting along, nostrils above the waterline, when the emergency phone rings. Paramedics are bringing a priority one patient – a security guard shot in the stomach during a robbery at a local bank. The dispatcher tells us that CPR is in progress. My heart sinks – CPR in a trauma patient means that Grim already has the upper hand.

The paramedics burst through the door. They are doing chest compressions and ventilating with a bag and mask. The patient is a thin young man, stripped to his underpants. We each take a corner of the sheet and move him across from the trolley to the bed. He is ice cold and there is not a vein in sight.

The algorithm for cardiac arrest is ABC, standing for airway, breathing and circulation. But I skip A and B and go straight to circulation. I guess where his femoral vein is and jab in a big-bore cannula. Pull back the plunger and advance at an angle. I'm in luck; dark blood trickles into the barrel of the syringe. I withdraw the needle, leaving the plastic cannula in place. Connect the drip and secure it with a clear plaster. Spin the wheel on the administration set to wide open.

That is all I can do for now to remedy the circulatory collapse, so I go back to A. When I open his mouth to intubate him, I see his tongue and mouth mucosa are a waxy white. He has no blood volume left. An easy airway, I slot the tube in place and secure it with tape. Then I step back to assess the patient. Two small wounds, no bigger than cigarette burns, one on his back and the other below his belly button on the front. The trajectory of the bullet must have hit one of his major arteries.

The AED gives instructions in a pseudo-American accent. The AED is an amazing invention; a little box that starts talking to you as soon as you open its lid. It can be found on the walls of airports and gyms and, of course, emergency departments. It is designed for use by the general public with no medical training and it tells you what to do with a patient in cardiac arrest.

'Analysing rhythm. Do not touch the patient.'

We all step back obediently.

'No shock advised. Continue CPR'

Tock tock tock, the machine keeps time for CPR.

The only way to help this patient would be to open his abdomen and clamp the bleeding artery. But no surgeon will take a patient to the theatre who is already in cardiac arrest. Too late, too late. I feel Grim's wry smile behind me. I am kneeling on the bed doing chest compressions. After 10 minutes of CPR, I decide to call it. I climb off, my scrubs sticking bloodily to my knees. I check his pupils and brain stem reflexes one more time and declare him dead. I feel sad and frustrated. What a waste of a life.

One of the paramedics has video footage of the shooting from a security camera on scene. The security guard runs towards the robbery and the robber raises the gun as if pointing a finger. There is no sound but the security guard jerks back and falls to the ground. The robber walks away, so calm that I wonder if he is on drugs. It is surreal to see this dead man, so alive not more than half an hour ago.

I am shaken. Seven years ago, I was shot in a robbery. I recall a tall man wearing brown gloves and an incredible jolt. Then I was on the floor and my whole body was humming, as if a swarm of bees had been let loose at my centre. There was no pain but the strong presence of my brother in the room. He lives far away but we are close and the thought 'this will ruin his day' flitted across my mind.

The robbers frisked me and ransacked my house. I held my breath and pretended to be dead. My right lung was blown away and my spine shattered by the bullet, but I had survived. I was paralysed at first but eventually recovered. I was lucky.

I look at this dead young man in his blue underpants. It is his unlucky day.

Fifteen

I don't want to sound like a Doomsday Prepper, but maybe all those people stockpiling baked beans and sardines knew something that I didn't.

Today I have discarded my plastic visor and replaced it with a watertight set of goggles. I am sure I look like an insect travelling in space.

A patient accuses us – the medical profession, and me, in particular – of not knowing what we are doing. She tested positive for coronavirus 14 days ago and was told to self-isolate at home and come into the hospital if she developed worsening symptoms. She was instructed to come back for a repeat swab in 14 days and now that she has waited in the queue and been treated like a pariah, she is told that she does not need another swab.

I admit openly that we don't know what we are doing, and she stares at me in amazement. It is the truth and I cannot deny it. Every day brings new guidelines and new chaos. The physician on call confided in me that she has never said 'I don't know' so many times in one day. This is highly unusual as, compared to the other specialties, physicians pride themselves on having all the answers.

I explain to the patient that we are not willfully wasting her time but that we must adhere to the National Institute for Communicable

Diseases – the NICD – guidelines. The guidelines have changed, and we are no longer repeating positive swabs at 14 days. When she recovers from the shock of my admission, we have a meaningful discussion and I think that she leaves the ED with a much clearer idea of how this pandemic has thrown us all off balance.

I am on the late shift and the night is sharp on the edges and deep in the middle. I bump the battered door of the ED with my shoulder and slither out through the gap. I have become adept at making my way around the hospital without actually touching anything.

Thousands of twinkling lights carpet the valley, silently sparkling in the autumn night. The tarmac is deserted, whispering wet from a midnight rain. I long for a cool, starry sky far from this blazing neon hub.

Reaching into my memory, I uncork an image of the ocean. Walking on the beach at sunrise, the sand brushed clean by the high tide. The water is almost oily in its stillness, the surface a copper blue sheen sliding over the swells. Before the wind picks up and feathers the surface, the waves seem smaller and more solemn. I can almost hear the slow sigh of the ocean on the shore.

An ambulance pulls into the bay, bringing me work. I follow the stretcher inside. It turns a corner and disappears into a room. Sometimes, I am a shadow, flitting across the threshold and flickering behind the curtains. Watching from the outside as the troubled river swirls by. Sometimes, I am the captain of the universe and the master of the underworld. At other times, I am deep in the water, buffeted and churned, desperate to stay afloat.

There are moments of quiet desolation and moments of exhilarating triumph.

The hands of the clock creep towards 5 am. We are through the witching hour,when it is said that the barrier between the physical and the spiritual realms is at its thinnest and most permeable.

The parking area is subdued in the half-light of dawn. Smokers huddle around a concrete ashtray despite a 'NO SMOKING' sign emblazoned across the doors. When the doors are open the big red capitals are split in two. I remember a baby born in ED being blessed with the name Nosmo King. We were perplexed, until his mother showed us the name appearing and disappearing as the double doors opened and closed. The name had a nice ring to it.

I skirt the haze of second-hand smoke and the nasty-looking stain on the paving. There is a little wall at the edge of a grassed area where I sometimes sit for time out from the ED. I call it the shirking wall. I would like to sit there now to watch the sky lighten, but there are patients waiting to be seen.

There is a hopeful hint of toast and coffee in the air. The early morning in the ED can be deserted in the aftermath of chaos but today the storm is still in full frenzy. Linen is crumpled, monitors chime and staff move around with focused urgency. The air hums with activity.

I put on the kettle. Set up my mug with a teabag. Two minutes past five, I pick up the next file from the in-tray. I see a family member standing in the corridor, arms folded. Never a good sign. I put on my mask and gloves.

'Finally. We have been waiting for two hours!'

I suppress an eye-roll. The time on the sticker is 4.25 am. The sticker is generated at the front desk as the patient arrives.

'Sorry about that.' Even to my own ears, I don't sound very sorry.

'Good morning,' I greet the patient in an attempt to dilute the irritation. Or perhaps to annoy him more – long nights can bring out the stranger in me. I suppress a sudden urge to burst into song. 'What can we help you with today?'

And so, the dance begins. Much more tolerable in the relative safety of daylight, but I still miss the beach.

Sixteen

It is day 12 of the lockdown and every time I come to work there is a new layer to don. Today I get a little cover for my neck, which protects the skin between my apron and the bottom of my mask. I have taken to having two hot baths every day with germicidal soap, but I still have not taken any chloroquine. The articles that supported it as prevention are now being replaced by negative statistics.

The numbers are definitely down, and it seems that people are taking serious heed of the lockdown and are only coming to the ED if it is absolutely necessary. In cubicle two there is a young lady who is half-sitting, half lying on the bed – perched awkwardly on one buttock. She is in severe discomfort and she looks like a genuine customer.

'I fell on a broom.' She tells me tearfully. I wait to hear more. 'It went up my bum.'

I find this an improbable story and send the family out so that I can talk to her alone.

'Tell me what really happened,' I ask, sitting down on the chair so that I am eye level with her.

'Really, doctor, that is what happened. You can ask my brother and my mother; they were in the kitchen with me. I climbed up on the counter to get a pot from the top of the cupboard. The broom was leaning up against the edge; I lost my balance and fell backwards on it.'

What bad luck, I think to myself. I call her mother back in to be with her for the examination.

The broom handle has torn through her rectal wall and her external anal sphincter. The sphincter, which is the circular muscle in charge of continence, is badly damaged. It is an especially important muscle and, I find out today, it is almost impossible to repair. I speak to three general surgeons before I am directed to a professor of colorectal surgery, who reluctantly agrees to take her on.

There is a moratorium on interhospital transfers in the pandemic. It will be a mountain of paperwork in order to get the broom victim from our hospital to a facility on the other side of town, where the professor works. I peel off my layers and make a cup of tea to help me wade through it. I wipe the phone after each call and my pen every time I pick it up. Then I wipe all the surfaces, and my stethoscope for good measure.

The tray of files waiting is full and I waste time counting them and looking at the main complaints. The next patient is an elderly, demented man who is literally covered in blood. It is smeared all over his face and body and his hair is stiff with it. He stares at me vacantly and I can't see any open wounds. With the risk of corona exposure, we are not letting any family come into the unit with the patients. I ask the staff and they rustle up a very disgruntled daughter.

'What happened to your dad?' I ask.

'His nose is bleeding,' she tells me in a bored tone, while looking at her phone. He is lying on his back, so the blood is probably running down the back of his throat for now.

I look at his list of medications and see that he is on Warfarin. Warfarin is a blood thinner, and was first discovered by the Wisconsin Alumni Research Foundation and named accordingly. It is a by-product of fungal growth on certain crops and was discovered after half the cattle in a large herd bled to death after minor procedures like de-horning. The cattle had eaten lucerne

which was contaminated with a fungal growth that made coumarin
– the blood thinner – as a by-product

It is the same chemical compound as rat poison.

It is not impossible for a human to bleed to death from a
nosebleed, especially an elderly one on Warfarin.

I pull blood to check Grandpa's haemoglobin and clotting
time. The daughter looks suspicious and asks why I am taking his
blood. I explain that I need to assess how much blood he has lost
and whether his blood is too thin on the Warfarin. She asks if it is
really necessary. I want to point out that I would not be doing the
investigations if they were not really necessary. There is nothing
in it for me – it's not like I'm going to sell his blood or drink it. In
fact, it is a hassle to have to look up all the results and act on them.
It would be easier not to do investigations.

I'm just trying to help him.

No 'out-loud' voice, I remind myself. It gets you into trouble.

I ask his daughter why he is on Warfarin.

'To thin his blood.' She looks at me like I am a complete moron.

'Yes, I know that,' I try to keep my voice level and patient, and
refrain from telling her that I did study that section at medical
school. 'But why does he need his blood thinned?'

'I don't know. Can't you look it up in his records?'

I don't say it, but I want to remind her that this is an Emergency
Department and every time you come here, it is supposed to be
an emergency. It is not a general practice, where we keep your file
and you ring up to get a repeat prescription. I don't mind if you
come in with a minor complaint which is not, strictly speaking, an
emergency. But we will need to take a full history with each visit.
I know this must be enormously tedious for you, because you are
very busy and important, but there it is.

I can see that I am not going to win the daughter over, so I shift
my focus to Grandpa. I explain that I am going to have to put packs
into his nose in order to stop it bleeding. He has no idea of who I
am or where I am, but he nods his head obligingly. I shove plugs

into both of his nostrils and inflate them with air. I hope that the plugs will squeeze the nasal septum between them and stop the bleeding.

I come back in five minutes to check on him. The blood is now dribbling out of the corners of his eyes, like bright red tears. It coats his eyeballs every time he blinks. He looks horrendous – like a special effect in a horror movie – and I dash off to call the ear, nose and throat specialist. He sounds as bored as the daughter and says it is quite common for the blood to back up into the tear ducts, but I can admit the patient if I like. This is music to my ears. I fill in the forms and send Grandpa off to the ward.

I wade through the rest of the shift in my goggles and mask and layers of plastic until it is time to get home to the snoopies.

Greyhounds, pointers and border collies are always on death row at the rescue organisations. They are a nice idea until they go berserk in the garden and destroy everything in their path. They dig up the plants, run bald tracks on the lawn and chew off your windscreen wipers. Soon they are surrendered to sit in a wire cage and stare mournfully out, waiting for the likes of me to come along.

Sadly, there are a lot more of them than there are of me. The good news is that corona seems not to infect animals. So far.

Some breeds of dog need more structure than others. Owning them is hard work, like having a job, as opposed to easier dogs that are an accessory, like a handbag, that you can leave at home unattended.

I once had a German Shorthaired Pointer – imaginatively named Brown Dog – who was a solid chocolate brown from the tip of her nose to her claws. Not a speck of white. On the day that she arrived, I realised that she loved to chase things. Balls, cars or livestock would do. The latter two were no match for a silky brown dog.

She had been out of the car for less than five minutes before she was off after a horse in the paddock. I yelled 'Brown Dog!' and she fell to the ground in a mock coma. She just lay there, her eyes open and her tongue lolling to the side. Over the years she repeated this performance every time I said 'Brown Dog' in anything other than a loving whisper. She must have had a guilty conscience.

I recounted the story to a young doctor colleague and 'Brown Dog' became our code name for patients who faked it. Patients who came in groaning and crying and pretending to be at death's door when there was nothing objectively wrong with them. It's a Brown Dog, we would say, rolling our eyes.

Of course, to confuse matters, Brown Dogs could also be objectively sick, and manage to deter our diagnostic skills with all manners of hysteria. The patients that make the least noise are usually the ones that are the sickest, but just because a patient is howling the place down, it doesn't mean that they aren't ill or injured. All it means is that their airway and breathing can be checked off as adequate on the ABC algorithm.

I take everyone seriously in the ED, so screaming and flailing about only serves to distract me rather than attract my attention. Similarly, patients who cover their head with the blanket or refuse to speak to me are not helpful. It just makes me want to ask, 'Why are you making it so difficult for me to help you?'

Years after Brown Dog had left us, I heard a registrar telling a colleague that the patient was a Brown Dog. I was amazed. Brown Dog was famous!

Seventeen

Humans should not climb onto roofs or ladders unless they have a harness or a set of wings.

It is day 13 of the lockdown and the evening before Good Friday. A woman brings her husband to the ED because he has spent the day drinking beer and painting the roof, probably more of the former than the latter. No one was holding the ladder, so it overbalanced and he fell about two metres from the roof onto the ground.

He is covered in paint and beer, an arctic white splash on the resus bed with blue eyes and pink lips. The sharp smell of paint mixed with the fermented beer is actually quite pleasant.

He has severe pain over the left side of his chest, where he landed against the upturned edge of the fallen ladder. I listen to his chest and think that he has decreased air entry on the left side.

I get a portable chest X-ray which looks normal.

I suspect that the radiologist is still in the hospital because I can see her car in the parking lot. She won't answer the internal phone on a Thursday evening before a public holiday, so I call her on her mobile. I tell her that I am worried that the painter has air or fluid collecting between his lung tissue and its lining. This can happen with stabbings or gunshots to the chest, where air is sucked from the environment through the hole and into the relative negative pressure of the thoracic cavity. It can also happen without an open wound, where broken ribs have punctured the lung.

85

The radiologist says that the chest X-ray is normal. No blood or air collection and no broken bones visible.

'He's a Brown Dog,' my colleague asserts as he walks by to see another patient.

The painter can't be faking what I hear with my stethoscope, so I send him down for a CT scan of his chest. Because I am worried, and because I need a break from the ED, I tag along and take the chest drain trolley with me.

While I am peering through the porthole window into the scanner, I see that the painter's condition is deteriorating. He is increasingly short of breath and his blood pressure is dropping. He tries to sit up and almost rolls off the metal tray that slides him into the scanning doughnut.

We stop the scan and I go in to reassess him. Despite his laboured breathing, there is definitely no air entry on his left.

The painter has a tension pneumothorax.

This is every ED doctor's nightmare. I am alone in the basement with a radiographer who looks about 10 years old and a patient who is going to die within the next minute if I don't do something. Air or blood is building up in the lining of his chest cavity, collapsing his lung and putting pressure on his heart. The algorithm dictates that I should decompress the tension with a needle, followed by a chest drain. But I don't have a needle with me; I only have the chest drain set.

The drain should be placed in the midline of the armpit, between the fourth and fifth rib. Ribs can only be counted in the middle, where they arise from the sternum, and then followed laterally. This is time-consuming and very difficult to do when a patient is suffocating in front of you.

I think of the surgery professor. 'If you have the time,' she had said, 'you can fuss about the placement of the drain. But if you are in a hurry, you can safely place the drain just below where the armpit hair would end.' She had solemnly placed a fingertip on a spot in an unsuspecting colleague's armpit.

I am in a hurry. The painter is gasping. I open the kit, put on the gloves and pick up the scalpel. I put my left index finger on the professor's spot, find the rib and aim to go over the top of it. The major vessels run underneath each rib and I want to steer clear of them. I stab the scalpel through the skin and the painter bellows in pain. I have skipped the local anaesthetic because there is none on the tray and there is no time to fetch it. I feel the resistance give as I enter the chest cavity and I follow the scalpel with my finger. Blood rushes out before I can get the rubber tube into the hole that I have made.

'Gosh,' I think, 'there's a lot of blood, especially as I thought it was a normal chest X-ray.' The radiographer's eyes are the size of saucers.

I hope that I haven't put the chest drain into his heart.

I use forceps to feed the pipe into the hole, secure the skin edges around it and connect it to the chest drain bottle, which is half-full of water. The professor used to call it an 'under-water drain', pronouncing it carefully, as if it should be performed by a special agent in scuba gear.

The image reminds me that I forgot my goggles in the ED. Hopefully, I won't contract any transmissible diseases from the painter.

Bubbles should appear as the trapped air escapes from the opening of the drain, which is under the surface of the water. The water meniscus should move up and down as the patient breathes, confirming that the tube is in the pleural space, where it should be, rather than an awful alternative, like the heart or the spleen.

The painter's bottle fills up with blood. I must clamp the tube and empty the bottle. I wonder if I can refill the water from the tap. The patient is stable enough now for me to Google this on my phone and the answer is no, it must be sterile water.

We finish the scan and make our way back to the ED. The few images that were captured before the drain was placed show more than a litre of blood in the left chest cavity with multiple broken ribs. The blood could not be seen on the chest X-ray as the painter was lying flat. The blood was spread out at the back of the lung, rather than collecting at the bottom and making a nice clean line as if the patient had been sitting or standing.

In my head I have thanked the professor hundreds of times for her advice. It is as if she walked this jungle in advance and gave me a map of where the dreadful terrors lurk. I remind myself to call her to enquire as to her wellbeing and hear what she thinks of the pandemic.

Eighteen

The good news is that it is Easter Friday morning; the bad news is that I am working. The greyhounds don't observe Easter but still, it feels a little depressing. I am bracing myself for chocolate overdoses and lacerations from poor gift-opening technique. It would have been day 15 of the lockdown; there would have been six days to go.

Last night, the president addressed the nation. He told us, in another articulate speech, that he had no choice but to extend the lockdown for an additional two weeks.

I agree that it is the right thing to do.

So, it is 21 days of lockdown, season two. Three whole weeks to go. Not that it affects my everyday life, as I am working as usual, but the restrictions on shopping and travelling are wearing us all down. I can't help thinking that it may be nature's revenge and people in quarantine are experiencing how animals may feel in a zoo. Perhaps even how bats and pangolins may have felt while on death row in a Chinese market.

Maybe the whole human race is going to have to take a hit for our appalling behaviour thus far.

I have painted white masks on the little chocolate bunnies that I have brought for the staff for today and Sunday. I watch them open them and eat them.

It seems that most people start with the ears.

The first patient of the day accidentally drank a bottle of Dettol.

She mistook it for her beer – at eight o'clock in the morning – and swigged it down. The Dettol had been in the original plastic bottle, not even decanted into a beer glass, so I ask about deliberate self-harm.

The patient burps and the room smells like a dressing tray. No, she just thought it was beer. Just to be safe, I call the poison centre. Who would have guessed, Dettol is very toxic when ingested. It can cause metabolic acidosis and the patient must go to ICU for hourly monitoring of her arterial blood gas. The physician on duty wishes me a happy Easter and miserably accepts the patient.

I am staring longingly at the shirking wall when the sisters call me to a patient with a prolapsed cord in the labour ward. The ED has the privilege of covering any emergency in the hospital, especially after hours when the admitting doctor is not in the ward. The umbilical cord was delivered first during this labour and it is getting compressed between the baby's head and the mother's pelvis, cutting off the blood supply to the baby.

I tell the patient to stop pushing and drop the head of the bed into the Trendelenburg position so that her head is lower than her feet. I must keep the baby's head out of the pelvis until it is delivered by emergency C-section. I get up onto the bed, between the patient's legs, and dial the gynaecologist on my mobile phone before putting my gloved hand into the patient's vagina and pushing the baby's head back inside. From this position I liaise with the gynaecologist and travel to theatre with the patient.

Later I hear the patient talking to her family in recovery. The labour was going well, she tells them, until the doctor did a vaginal exam. Her hand got stuck inside and the patient had to have an operation to have it removed.

In all the excitement, I had clearly not explained the situation to the patient.

Back in the ED I find an unhappy-looking couple waiting. The man is sitting on the bed, so he is probably the patient, but the lady looks more upset. There is no presenting complaint on the front of the file, so I ask how I can help them. The lady motions for me to close the door even though the department is completely deserted, and the sisters are all in the tearoom, feasting on an Easter lunch. This cubicle has a problem with the door and, if you slide it too far, it doesn't open again. I don't want to spend Easter Friday locked in a cubicle, so I slide the door half way shut.

'I think I have broken my penis,' the man tells me ruefully. The lady starts to cry and wrings her hands. During morning sex he 'mis-aimed', he says, and bumped it hard against his wife's pubis. I have heard about a fractured penis in theory but have never actually seen one.

It looks awful, with a gruesome bend halfway up the shaft, terrible bruising and blood oozing from the urethra. It is not a bone, of course, so it isn't technically a fracture, but one or more of the three columns of fluid that create an erection have ruptured. He will need to see a urologist and may need surgery. I ask his permission to send an image to the specialist. He consents and I take a few photos, select one and WhatsApp it to the urologist on call.

I make some tea and send a few happy Easter messages to family and friends, but I hear nothing back from the urologist. I call her and, after brief formalities, I ask her if she saw the picture yet. No, she says, what picture?

I go cold. Where have I sent the image? My mind flashes back to the neighbourhood security group and all the Covid doctor groups that I have visited this morning – did I post a picture of a mutilated penis on one of these groups?

'Hang on a second,' I tell her, and put the call on hold. Desperately I scroll back through my messages. There is the image, sent to her old mobile number. I thank the universe and vow never to send a sensitive image again. Fortunately the man didn't need surgery.

There is a lull for a few minutes, and I go outside to sit on my wall. April in Johannesburg is a spectacular month and the morning is clean and hopeful. The car park is empty and there is almost no traffic, until a car pulls up with the hazards flashing. A young woman is passed out in the back seat. The car is hammered, with rust spots on the bodywork and the mirrors held on with duct tape. The driver of the car has more tattoos than teeth, which is a ratio that I have previously noted, and am sure would yield some solid research. The patient is out cold and, as we get her out of the car, I have to ask the question.

'Is she on medical aid?'

Of course not.

The government hospital is 10 minutes down the road. One day in a private hospital ICU will cost more than I earn in a month. But I am tired of arguing with people and trying to save them money. I have learned the hard way that no act of kindness goes unpunished. Trying to change the rules to suit the timeframe or budget of the patient is a singularly bad idea.

So, we drag the unconscious woman out of the back seat and onto the first bed in resus. She is probably a combination of alcohol and the ubiquitous Easter overdose, intentional or accidental.

The level of consciousness in an unresponsive person is first assessed by saying something – preferably their name – loudly and in close proximity.

'What's her name?' I ask Mr Tattoo. He tells me and I shout it into her ear, simultaneously pinching and rubbing the skin in the middle of the chest. This painful stimulus, called a sternal rub, usually elicits eye opening. No luck in this lady, so I prise her eyelids open. Truly unconscious people have a laxity of their lids that is missing in Ms Tattoo. She allows me to open her eyes but with very slight resistance. I think that she is pretending. Her pupils are slightly dilated, and her conjunctiva are red.

I lift the arm closest to me so that her hand is directly above her face and drop it. Usually people who are pretending to be unconscious will not let their hand fall onto their face. Ms Tattoo's inky arm finds its way back to the bed without damaging anything.

We hook her up to the monitors and the vital signs are normal.

Level of consciousness is assessed by scoring the patient on the Glasgow Coma Scale. This uses eye opening, verbal and motor response in response to verbal and painful stimuli. If someone does not respond at all verbally, does not open their eyes to voice command and doesn't move away from a painful stimulus, they score one for each of the three. Three is the lowest score that you can get – essentially it means that the patient is deeply unconscious or dead.

My next trick to wake her up will be a drip, blood tests and a catheter. I ask the sister for an 'in and out' catheter so that I can get urine to check for recreational drugs. I don't want an indwelling catheter as I have another trick up my sleeve.

The drug test urine cup lights up like a child's eyes at an Easter feast. I ask Mr Tattoo about substances. She uses cat and smokes weed but nothing serious. I wonder what would rank as a serious drug. Heroin perhaps, although the opioid stripe in the uricup is positive too.

I fetch a bottle of ethyl chloride, a volatile liquid that we spray on the skin to numb it for procedures. It is painfully cold, and I squirt it on her earlobe. Nothing – her eyes stay closed. I find that most fakely unconscious patients close their eyes. Unrousable people with open eyes are usually a quarter to dead. I suppose it is hard to keep a straight face as curious medical staff move in and out of your field of vision.

I am going to have to do blood tests and a CT scan of her brain. I hope that they have the cash.

While she is in the CT scanner, I see a young man who stabbed himself in the thumb with a pair of scissors while opening a box of chocolates. I tell him that I have been expecting him and he looks perplexed. He has an arterial bleed which squirts furiously when I remove the plastic shopping bag that he has tied around his wrist. The sister faints while trying to swab for me and I must finish tying off the bleeder on my own.

The next patient is triaged as an emergency and comes

through without a file. In the space for the main complaint it says 'poisoning' and the young lady tells me anxiously that she ate a weasel. I wonder if this is some horrendous Easter ritual until she embellishes that she had already finished the pancake when she saw them in the flour. I realise that she means a weevil and reassure her that they are completely harmless. By now Ms Tattoo is back from the CT scanner and the scan is normal. I write up 20 milligrams of intravenous diuretic. Half an hour passes, and her eyes fly open.

'I need to pee!'

It works, almost every time. Nothing works every time.

Nineteen

Like Groundhog Day, we are back on day two of lockdown. We are learning important lessons and it seems that we can live without alcohol and takeaways. Nature is regenerating without human interference and they say there are dolphins in the canals in Venice.

It is my first day off in almost a month and I am not really sure what to do with myself. I have a dozen projects on the farm but all of them require that I buy something – a tin of paint or a tap washer – in order to complete them. As all the shops are closed, it narrows my options significantly.

I need to have a day away from the 'Coro Coro', but I can't help opening an interesting article posted on one of the groups. I read it at the kitchen table over a steaming mug of coffee.

The article proposes that the Coronavirus19 has a high mortality rate because the virus makes a protein that attaches to haemoglobin in the blood and pushes the oxygen off. The purpose of the red blood cell in the human body is to carry oxygen around and so, when the oxygen is pushed off the taxi, so to speak, multiple things happen.

If the red cell cannot carry oxygen, the level of oxygen being delivered to the tissues will drop and the person will become hypoxic. We know about hypoxia from our Hs and Ts and it is not a good thing. Also, the empty circulating red cells confuse the body, and the liver and spleen will begin destroying them, resulting in the accumulation of various toxins. The bone marrow is simultaneously driven to make more red cells.

But there is also the important effect of the displaced oxygen. When oxygen is bored – in other words it is not busy binding to something or being used in a chemical reaction, it can become a free radical.

A free radical sounds innocuous, like a bearded student smoking weed, but is a dangerous thing. It is an atom with an extra electron and because electrons like to be in pairs, free radicals scavenge the body looking for available electrons with which to pair. They do a lot of damage as they go; an attractive, charismatic individual loosed on a community of established couples.

Then there is the problem of the iron. In mammalian blood, and elsewhere in nature, there is a protein called haeme. Haeme is made up of a little chemical ring called porphyrin with an atom of iron at its centre, making up a small basket in which to carry essential gases like oxygen and carbon dioxide. Haeme is bound to a larger protein called globin, and four haemes with their associated globin proteins make up one haemoglobin molecule. Haemoglobin makes up most of the bulk of the red blood cell.

This article suggests that the virus may attach to the porphyrin ring of haemoglobin, knocking the oxygen off but also releasing free iron into the body and the lungs. The iron itself could account for the cascade of respiratory and organ failure that we are seeing in advanced Covid-19 illness.

I read the article through again. It is an interesting postulation. We have all been chasing the coronavirus as primarily a lung problem and the article suggests that it is actually a problem with the red blood cells and that the lung damage is collateral. This opens the possibility that there are treatment options other than ventilation and also may explain why ventilation, alone, is not very successful. It would also explain how chloroquine may help in treating the virus. Initial reports said that this was an incidental association as chloroquine treats malaria, which is a parasite and has a completely different mechanism of action to a virus. But malaria also attacks the red blood cells and chloroquine prevents the parasites' access to the protein part of haemoglobin.

I think about the implications of this while I work in the garden. The snoopies laze around while I struggle with the jungle that has grown wild with all the late summer rain. Vines and branches are choking out my precious roses.

By lunchtime I am exhausted and need to rest by the pool. The snoopies relocate and have a swim. Autumn gives the air a sharpness, but the sky is still a deep summer blue. I sit under the canopy of a giant marula tree and wonder if it is time to retire from medicine. I think I should leave on a high note, before I become the old codger who is a liability to the unit.

I think back on my medical career. I worked without respite for four full years after finishing my training. I was swamped in debt and there was no way to rescue myself other than working ridiculously long hours. Ten years after starting medical school, I took a week off. I went to the ocean and lay on a jetty as the sea surged beneath the planks and the universe wheeled overhead. I greeted my old friends in the night sky – the Southern Cross, Orion's belt and all the familiar constellations. The stars were bright and close and looked the same as they had when I lay on the night-time lawn as a child on our farm in Limpopo. I had loved the shrill crickets surging around me and the absolute darkness of the mountains where they met the brilliant starry sky.

With regret I realised how many days and nights had passed me by as I chased my dream of becoming a doctor. I was quiet inside for the first time in what felt like forever and I saw that my life had been in constant motion. I was not sure if I had been chasing or being chased but I had been so focused on my goal that I had not seen the world around me for 10 long years.

The bay was a magical crescent – satin black under a cold, white moon. Lacy lines of fluorescent surf flared and faded. Beyond the line of breakers, the ocean glimmered in the starlight. The waves were small and lazy, rushing onto the sand.

I stood ankle-deep as the hissing water seeped away, bathed in the vastness of the ocean and sky. I wondered if the creatures beneath the surface could see the thousands of glittering stars above and whether they followed the arc of the sun and the wide silver path beneath the rising moon.

I think back on that night when I feel like I am losing track of stillness and reflection, when I feel too caught up in the chase. Sometimes the chaos of the ED overwhelms me, and I step back to the surge of the ocean and the vastness of the universe around me.

As I sit in the garden and watch the daylight fade, I consider what it would mean for me to leave the ED. Maybe sell the farm and move to the beach. The ocean feels a long way from here.

The snoopies stretch and yawn. The sun is sinking in the west and I take them for a long walk through the twilit fields. The moon rises almost full, a luminous white disc in the sky.

When we walk home it is dark. The dikkops fly up in the moonlight, their wings a blur and their sharp call breaking the silent night, three sharp whistles over and over. Paperbark trees show their white flakes in brilliant relief and the fever trees are glowing.

The evening is warm and magical – perfect for playing the cello. It is the closest instrument to the human voice and the low vibration of the strings lifts my heart in an inexplicable way. Music transcends my everyday life and it helps me to forget about hypoxia and ventilators and lethal germs teeming everywhere.

The music curls around the farmhouse and out of the open doors and windows. A steady pull and slide, humming and purring under my touch. The gleaming cello sings to the silent furniture and polished floor. A breeze rustles the leaves in huge trees outside and shuffles the sheet music on the stand. It feels like the universe is breathing deeply.

The night is humid, and my shirt is damp and still stained from the garden. I play on – Pachelbel's Canon in D major and then Bach's first cello concerto. Up and down, my fingers pressing and releasing, the bow smooth and taut. The slow, throaty notes consume me. There is no place for Grim here, no illnesses or gruesome injuries. There is only the throb of liquid gold flowing out of the house and into the dark night beyond.

The greyhounds sleep on, undisturbed. I wonder if dogs appreciate music. The slumbering pack are scattered about on their beds, their rib cages rising and falling rhythmically. Some of their muzzles are completely grey and their eyes are white with cataracts. The old ones know the resting places on the walks and the short-cuts home. But they still look forward to their walks and their biscuits before bed and I'm sure their dreams are as rich, if not richer, than ours.

Twenty

It is two in the morning on Easter Monday and we are deep in the witching hour. All bets are off, and anything can happen. To add to my woes, we have scraped the bottom of the staffing barrel tonight. The nursing team doesn't fill me with confidence..

There is an elderly lady – I'm sure hauled out of retirement for the public holiday – with only one tooth and a jittery young man with a shaved head who looks like he is fond of the devil's sugar. We are two short, so the locum agency has sent a young nurse aide who looks terrified out of her wits and repeats everything that I say. The receptionist is moribund – I have not seen him move a muscle for hours – but somehow the files are being generated from inside his cubicle.

Tonight, the South African figures are 2028 positive cases and 25 deaths which is a mortality rate of 1.2 per cent. This is significantly better than the global figure which is close to six per cent and I am feeling a tiny flicker of hope.

On the downside, the groups are flooded with opinions debunking the haemoglobin postulate. It seems the article was written by an imposter under a pseudonym and now it has been removed from the blog. One particularly good article takes the theory apart step by step, pointing out numerous factual and scientific flaws. I have to agree with the logic that the author of the new article presents, and it seems that we are back to the theory that coronavirus attacks and destroys the alveoli in the lung.

The Easter weekend has been quiet with the lockdown but tonight the ED is a real dog and pony show.

The doorbell is set at a hateful pitch, and it keeps on chiming. Ambulance after ambulance rolls in; all the beds are occupied, and the waiting room is full of drunk people in feather boas and cowboy hats who are accompanying a teenager who fell off a balcony. They are buzzing despite the lockdown. Alcohol is brain Tippex and no one can recall how or why he fell. They found him in the car park and both his legs are broken. They are all drunk enough to find the situation hysterical.

A mother comes striding through the double doors, her daughter in her arms. Her whole demeanour is humming with stress.

'My baby is having an allergic reaction!'

'Allergic reaction,' the nurse aide announces.

The child looks about five, so she is hardly a baby, but her eyes are swollen, and she is scratching at raised welts on her neck. Devil's Sugar takes her straight through to the resus room and I follow.

'What is she allergic to?' I ask.

'Peanuts,' her mother replies.

'Peanuts,' the nurse aide echoes.

'We were eating pesto,' the mom adds, and I glare at the nurse aide. She stares back, a rabbit in the headlights.

Pine nuts, commonly used in pesto, are tree nuts and are slightly different on the allergy spectrum to peanuts, but they are still nuts. Devil's Sugar is staring alternately at me and the patient, but he is in screen-saver mode. I can see that there will be no help from that quarter.

I wondered why they were eating pesto at three in the morning. I go to lift the little girl onto the bed, but she shoves me away.

'You need to get up on the bed, sweetie, so that I can have a look at you.'

'No. I don't want to,' the little girl asserts.

'Will you let the doctor take a look at you?' Mom asks in a wheedling tone.

I am not in favour of parents asking their children's permission for examination and treatment during an emergency. I understand that there is a strong move to empower children and teach them to find their own voice, but when your five-year-old is having an allergic reaction, you can't ask her to direct the process.

Nut allergies are a profoundly serious business. Years ago, I saw a teenager who dropped dead after her first kiss. Despite our best efforts, it was an unsuccessful resuscitation. It turned out that she was allergic to peanuts and her new boyfriend had eaten a peanut butter sandwich earlier in the day.

There is no weight written on the front of the file because the child refused to stand on the scale in triage. It is almost impossible to weigh an unwilling child, so I guess her weight using a formula of double her age plus eight. She is five, so her weight should be around 18 kilograms. I work out the dose of antihistamine and cortisone and send Devil's Sugar to fetch it.

I wrestle the child onto the bed so that I can check her airway and breathing. Luckily, it looks like this allergy is a skin reaction only; there is no wheezing or swelling of the airway. We give her the medication and I tell the mom that she will have to stay in the unit for observation for at least an hour. If her symptoms get worse, she will need an injection of adrenaline into her thigh muscle and a drip.

The little princess sits on the bed, ordering the nurse aide and her mother around, until her father arrives. He is livid and tells me that this is the third time in the past few months that his daughter has had to come to the ED because his ex-wife is completely irresponsible as regards her allergies. He wants to open a case of negligence against her and demands a copy of all the records.

It is a dismal family situation and I feel sorry for the little princess.

By 5 am it feels like the night will never end. The doorbell rings, the doors swing open and I glance outside to the grey light of dawn. The paramedics offload a very old lady on a spine board with head blocks stabilising her neck. She is as thin as a stick and her satin pajamas are saturated with blood. Her tearful daughter tells me that she fell asleep in front of the television and so only checked on her mother just after three. She found her unconscious in a pool of blood.

I assess granny. She has a genuine GCS of three, with a fixed gaze and no pupil response. If she weren't breathing steadily, I would think she was dead.

'She is unconscious, isn't she?' Her daughter asks anxiously.

'Yes, I'm afraid she is,' I answer. I think that it is pretty obvious that she is unconscious, but I try to be kind. The daughter is distraught and, to be honest, things aren't looking good for granny right now. I pat the daughter's shoulder and ask her to go and open a file.

I turn to address my nursing team and find them gathered in the corner like sheep in the presence of a predator.

'Let's log roll her off the spine board and see where she is bleeding from.'

'Log roll,' the nurse aide bleats but none of them move. I beckon them closer. 'We will need water and a cloth so that we can wash the blood off when we roll her and see where she's bleeding from.'

'Water and cloth.' It sounds like the nurse aide has never heard of such a notion, but the instruction triggers a distant memory for Senior Citizen, and she is set in motion. Soon a bucket on wheels appears and we roll granny on her side, keeping her head and spine aligned, in case she has a spinal injury.

Devil's Sugar oversees her head and his hands are shaking so badly that he dislodges granny's dentures. They would have had to come out anyway, but I hope he hasn't dislodged her spinal cord too. The nurse aide washes the blood off, and we roll granny back. There are no open wounds; she is bleeding from inside her left ear and her nose.

The blood is mixed with straw-coloured cerebro-spinal fluid, which is not a good sign. I think she has fractured her skull from a fall and is bleeding from her brain. The CT scan will confirm this, but first we need to heed the algorithm and attend to her airway and breathing. A trauma patient with a GCS less than eight is not able to protect their own airway. I hold an oxygen mask over her face.

'Ok, let's suction her airway and prepare for intubation.'

'Suction.' The nurse aide repeats; her eyes darting about. I want to shake her. 'Yes, suction. There, on the wall. Pass it to me.'

Senior Citizen comes to the rescue and hooks up the suction. I open granny's mouth and look in – there is a lake of blood at the back of her throat. How she is not choking and gurgling is a mystery.

The suction doesn't work. Senior Citizen has taken the initiative to put up a drip – she is getting into the swing of things – so I have to let go of the airway in order to fix the suction. Devil's Sugar is nowhere to be seen and the nurse aide is next to useless so it's up to Senior Citizen and me to save this granny from Grim.

We do a pretty good job, I think. Within an hour we have put her on a ventilator, scanned her brain, done blood tests and got her to ICU under the neurosurgeon. Against all odds, Granny has made it through the night, and I congratulate Senior Citizen on her work.

She beams with her one tooth and that makes me happy.

Twenty-One

The next patient is channelling Jackie Onassis. She is wearing a headscarf and dark glasses and is reclining in a regal pose. She tells me that she has had vomiting and diarrhea for a few hours and that she is definitely dehydrated. She needs a drip and a test for coronavirus.

I examine her and her hydration is fine. She is adamant about the drip so I might as well take some blood to prove to her that she is not dehydrated. We can give her some intravenous fluids with Zofran for nausea while we wait for the results. I reassure her that she does not need the coronavirus test as she has no respiratory symptoms at all.

When I come back to check on her, she is googling bacterial meningitis. She thinks she might have it, as she has had a headache for five days.

I tell her that if she had had bacterial meningitis for five days, she would be dead.

'What about a brain tumour?' she enquires, undeterred. She has a list of possible diagnoses from Dr Google. They are all sinister and highly unlikely.

'Anyway, I will need to be checked in,' she informs me.

'Checked in?' I ask, wondering if she has confused the ED with a hotel. People sometimes check out, but we don't check them in.

'You know, admitted,' she says, waving her hand towards the main hospital building. 'I am only on a hospital plan, so all of this,' she indicates the drip upon which she insisted, 'will not be covered by my medical aid unless I am admitted to the hospital.'

I start to explain to her that we cannot admit patients without a justified reason, but all hell breaks loose before I can get past the first sentence. There is shouting from the triage room and four nurses burst through the door, each holding a limb of an unconscious young man. His head and body hang in a limp sling between them. For some reason I am reminded of people carrying a dead tiger in the jungle. Not that I have ever seen a tiger, dead or alive, but there is something reminiscent in the floppy weight of his body.

No need for GCS and assessment tricks here; this guy is navy blue and clearly not breathing. Overdose, I think, with respiratory arrest. I leave Jackie and hurry to the resus room, where the sisters are heaving the bearded, blue guy onto the bed. They have put him the wrong way around so his head is under the little table at the bottom, but I think that this is the best that they can manage.

We are all struggling to get into aprons and gloves and goggles, and I am reminded of a post that told us there are no emergencies in a pandemic that are worth risking your life for. If you can't protect yourself, don't go near the patient.

The image of a gecko flashes through my mind as his head is so much bluer than the rest of his body. It looks like he has been strangled and I check his neck for a ligature while feeling for a pulse.

Neither is present.

Airway is the priority here and the sister starts chest compressions while I connect the oxygen to the bag mask valve and give two breaths. We must clip the table off the foot of the bed, release the brake and turn the bed around as the oxygen tubing is not long enough to reach, but it is easier than lifting the patient.

After two cycles of CPR he is less blue and is starting to make breathing efforts. I hand the ventilation bag to the sister and go to the waiting room to get some history.

It turns out that Bluebeard is severely asthmatic and has been struggling with shortness of breath for the past few weeks. He has been using his inhaler, but he became progressively distressed today and asked his girlfriend to bring him to the ED.

He stopped breathing two blocks away from the hospital.

We put him on a high flow oxygen nebuliser. Soon he is able to speak in short sentences, but he is gripping the cot sides to support his respiration. I listen to his chest and hear a faint wheeze. I would have preferred a loud wheeze as a silent chest is a dire situation in an asthmatic. It means that he is moving so little air that there is no sound.

Having woken him up with oxygen and CPR, we are now going to have to put him back to sleep and onto a ventilator. This guy is not going to cope on his own and to play a waiting game in the ICU is just asking for trouble. There is a junior doctor working the night shift and asthmatics are notoriously difficult to ventilate because of their high airway pressures. Additionally, Bluebeard has a short, thick neck which can make intubation a nightmare.

The best way to fix a problem is to prevent it happening, and I am not leaving a junior colleague to resuscitate Bluebeard at midnight when he crashes in ICU.

Once we stabilise him, I return to see Jackie. She is still googling, with her head scarf and shades in place. Her blood tests are back and, much to her surprise, they are all completely normal. She won't be checking in after all.

Dr Google is no good for prescribing medication or giving a sick note, both of which she wants. Which is a good thing, as it means that I will be gainfully employed for another few years.

Google will drive you crazy by suggesting all kinds of unlikely and catastrophic diagnoses. In my experience, we seldom predict the things that actually do go wrong, and rather spend our lives worrying about random things that don't.

A year ago, we would never have dreamed we would find ourselves in the midst of a pandemic. We have known about coronavirus for about 30 years, but this mutation has swept across the globe, decimating countries in its path. The germ with the halo, like a shimmering crown, has struck terror and chaos into the heart of the modern world. It seems more contagious than any virus before it, remaining alive outside the human body for weeks and infecting people at a lightning pace.

Like a world war, coronavirus will leave us forever changed.

I hope that the change will be for the better.

Twenty-Two

The pandemic is not going as planned.

We had a scrabble to get ready. We thought we would be facing a deluge of patients, a tidal wave of the dead and dying sweeping over us. I am sure the wave is yet to come but, at the moment, the numbers in the Emergency Department are right down. We have seen patients with Covid-19 and had some admissions with severe pneumonia. We have had a few scares and nearly lost a few people, but it is nothing like we expected.

It feels like nature is playing a trick on us. Coronavirus is playing hide and seek, calling 'Coming, ready or not,' and then hiding in the dark for a little bit longer. It is toying with us and waiting to catch us unawares. When we lose interest and drop our guard, I suspect that it is going to pounce.

Of course, I am attributing a conscious will to the virus when, in fact, I don't think it cares about us at all. The human race is just a vehicle for its own multiplication. It had better slow down, though, because if we all die from the virus then it will die too. Unless it makes another mutation and finds another host. Viruses are very clever little fragments of protein.

In the past six months it has managed to infect two and a half million people across the globe and that number is increasing exponentially.

Theories and graphs abound. Do we have some herd immunity in South Africa because of the tuberculosis vaccine? Is our curve flattened because we are not testing enough people? What will happen when the virus gets into our huge community of immunocompromised people? Will they be better off than immunocompetent people because they will not have the massive inflammatory surge that seems to kill people?

We don't know. Time will tell, I suppose. It is day 4 of our second lockdown and the number of infected people is 2415. It seems to go up by about 140 people per day and the logarithmic graph doesn't look too bad.

A few weeks ago the ED was completely crazy, with hundreds of people panicking about the virus. Now it is weirdly quiet, like the lull before the storm. People are staying home in the lockdown and only coming in if they have amputated their fingers with DIY gone wrong or have broken their leg and the bone is sticking through the skin. The rest of the usual customers are obeying the lockdown and staying home.

The question is, what has happened to all of them? Are they not coming in because they are scared to be exposed to the virus? I can understand the number of road traffic accidents being reduced because of the lockdown and also the ban on the sale of alcohol. But surely people are still having heart attacks and strokes and acute asthma.

So where are those patients?

The lockdown has not deterred a worried mother and father, who are standing over a small baby in a pink babygrow.

'I think she has broken her leg.'

I look at the baby and her sticker. She is three months old.

'Did you drop her?' I ask. They look horrified. 'By accident,' I add hastily.

'No. But every time we move her right leg, she cries.'

It is eight in the morning. I look at the pink–clad baby. She is smiling and waving her limbs in a healthy fashion. I play with her a bit and then straighten her legs one at a time. Sure enough, as I straighten the right leg, the smile turns into an instant cry.

'When did it start?' I ask. With no history of trauma, I am starting to think of septic arthritis and other sinister diagnoses.

'Last night after we put her down to sleep.'

A good general rule in the ED is to examine every patient properly. This entails exposing the area concerned and actually touching it. I always tell student doctors that the history is most of the diagnosis, but you can't get away without putting your hands on naked skin.

At least I don't think this baby has the virus.

I follow my own advice and take off the clothing to look at the leg in question. Looped around the foot is a thread from the upper legging of the babygrow. Every time we straighten her leg, the thread cuts in between her toes and she cries. I look at her parents.

'It's this thread between her toes.' We all laugh with relief, I snip off the thread and the problem is solved.

When it is busy at least the time passes quickly. Today time is dragging by as the patients come through in slow motion.

I am staring out of the window, into the ambulance bay. It is a miserable, rainy day. The world feels like an alien place and these grey skies day after day are wearing me down. The rain blurs the windows and gusts of wind jostle the weeping trees.

An ambulance reverses into the bay, red lights clotting on the shiny tarmac. The paramedics open the rear doors and I see a white head of hair strapped with crepe bandages. Up the ramp she comes, past the shirking wall with the view of the smokers. Today my wall and the smoking zone are abandoned. The paramedics offload granny onto a bed and give me the history.

'She had skin cancer removed a month ago at the dermatologist. The nurses in the frail care unit do the dressings three times a week but today it is bleeding a lot.'

She is 92 with watery blue eyes watching me from under multiple layers of gauze and crepe. I put on gloves and start peeling off the layers. The pads of gauze closest to her scalp are saturated with blood. Four weeks seems a long time after a procedure to be bleeding. When I lift the last layer, I find a deep hole on the top of her head. The blood wells up steadily. I put on fresh gauze and a pressure dressing. Over the next 10 minutes the blood stain appears on the outer layer of the crepe bandage. I remove it and re-assess the wound.

It is about five centimetres in diameter and quite mushy in the centre. I am reluctant to try and catch the bleeder with a suture. I sprinkle some adrenaline on a gauze swab and pack it into the wound. Placing another few layers, I reapply the pressure dressing and then take blood for a haemoglobin level and put up a drip to give cyklokapron. Properly called tranexamic acid, this blocks the production of plasmin and so helps the patient to clot. Her blood pressure is still acceptable, but she is elderly and has lost quite a lot of blood, so I speak to the physician about admission. He sounds long suffering.

'Hi. Calling from the ED; do you have a minute for me?'

'For you, always,' he answers smoothly. He is known as a hard sell for admissions, so I am well pleased to elicit this response.

'I have this 92-year-old lady...'

'Minute's up!' He interrupts.

'No!' I suppress a laugh. The physician is a genuinely kind man and takes granny without further ado.

When I meet him later in the ward, he tells me that granny's blood pressure soared up after admission. She was still oozing from the wound and he sent her for a CT scan. He shows me the images and I cannot believe what I see.

The skin lesion that the dermatologist removed went right down to the skull. Each time they pulled the dressing off, a little piece of skull came with it. The dressing that caused her admission had pulled off the last fragment of skull and tore the membrane around her brain. This opened the venous sinus which is a massive lake of blood at the top of the brain between the hemispheres. That mushy hole was her brain itself – just as well I didn't try to stitch it. When I put the adrenaline-soaked dressing on the open wound, it was absorbed directly into her bloodstream, causing her blood pressure to hurtle up.

She had bled her haemoglobin down to only three units by the time the physician managed to get the bleeding under control and start a transfusion. Despite being so alert and seemingly stable, granny had been holding hands with Grim and I had been none the wiser.

Twenty-Three

22 April 2020

There is an active debate about whether we should have had lockdown and social distancing at all or whether we should allow the virus to spread unhindered, burn itself out and wait for communities to develop herd immunity. Questions abound about how and when the lockdown is going to end and how we will keep afloat economically. The government is losing out on billions in tax and fuel levies and is now trying to distribute food parcels to poor communities that cannot work in lockdown. Many people have lost their jobs and, if the situation continues, things will worsen. It seems that about half the population can work from home, but the other half – like baristas and hairdressers – look set to take a hard knock.

The mortality rate worldwide is about 6 per cent. It is pretty hard for any government to turn their back on that and wait for herd immunity. It seems inhumane to stand by passively and let people get sick. Some trials are saying that 80 per cent of the population will be infected if no systems are put in place to limit the spread. If only 60 per cent of the 58 million people in South Africa were infected, that would be almost 35 million people. If 6 per cent of these people die, that would amount to approximately 2 million people. That is a lot of dead people. Just on a practical note, what would we do with all the bodies?

These are crazy times.

On my way to the hospital I am stopped in a roadblock. The

police officer leaps out of the half-light of dawn and I must jam on brakes in order not to run her down. I tell her that if she continues to jump out at people like that, I will be seeing her in the ED as a patient. This gets us off on the wrong foot, I suppose. She asks me where I am going and demands my letter of authority to travel and my driver's license. I ask her not to touch them and she tells me, scathingly, that she is wearing gloves. I point out to her that if she has been wearing the same pair of gloves all shift she might as well not bother. She takes my license with her and pins it under the clamp on her clipboard while she circles my car. I time my drive to work quite carefully and the 10 minutes on the side of the road makes me late.

I have never doubted my love for medicine, but I am discovering that being a healthcare worker is not an ideal career during a pandemic. Aside from the obvious and inevitable exposure to the dreaded germ, there is a slow-down in all medical services aside from managing patients with active Covid disease. This means that all other patients are staying away and that makes it very difficult to make a living.

Another problem is that, if we are exposed to a patient with definite coronavirus, we are quarantined for 14 days. This is not negotiable, but it is not covered as sick leave, unless we are actually sick. And quarantine without illness is expressly not covered by professional income protection plans. Which means that we must go home and not earn any money for 14 days. And, on our first day back, we could be exposed again.

All of these factors are poisoning my romance with medicine.

When I was growing up, we had a post box for mail collection. I loved getting it. In the daytime, the hall echoed with voices and the ritual pounding of stamps on ink trays and papers. When you opened the little steel door of the box, you could look through the hole and view the inner workings of the post office. As a child I found this strangely entertaining. With naive simplicity, I aspired to become an actress; but a secret agent was also a possibility. In retrospect, I am glad that none of the postal workers jabbed a sharp object though my spy hole and into my eye.

After applying to medical school, I checked for post every day. For weeks there was nothing. But then one evening I checked behind the box and there it was. The envelope with the crest of the University of the Witwatersrand on the front and a stamp from the medical school at the back. It was a thin letter, folded inside so that my name and address appeared in a clear window at the front.

I locked the post box and put the key in my pocket. My heart was hammering. I felt that I should perform some kind of ritual for luck, but the rational part of my brain told me that the letter said what it said; it said what it had said a few days ago and it reflected a decision made a few weeks ago at my interview. It was too late for lucky omens. I put my finger under the flap and opened it. I held my breath.

'We are pleased to inform you...'

Yes!

The rest of the letter was an elated blur. I turned my face to the panelled ceiling and said, 'Thank you, universe!'

I was in. I was going to be a doctor. It never occurred to me that I might not make it. Where I would live, whether I would pass, how I would survive without a salary – none of those things counted. In my head, it was just a matter of time.

I would trade six years of my life for a medical degree, and then another two in service to the government.

When I think back on that time, it is clear to me that things exist at least twice. Once in the head of their creator, and once in reality. I was so determined to become a doctor that the only hurdle was to get into medical school. Once I had gained access to that pathway, the end point existed so clearly in my consciousness that, barring a disaster, it had to happen.

I just had to spend my time wisely and do what I was told.

We had an ancient copy of *The Family Doctor* which, as a child, I read from cover to cover. It was bound in cracked red leather with pages so well worn that they were buttery to the touch. I memorised the signs and symptoms of every illness. Children are usually observant, and I think that I was more observant than most. I was certainly much more observant than I am as an adult. But my understanding and attribution of what I observed was often flawed and my world was skewed to my perspective only. I picked up on negative sentiment and possible danger, but my understanding of where it came from, and why, was often inaccurate.

I was ever vigilant for poisonous spiders, early symptoms of lockjaw or blood poisoning.

Armed with my knowledge from *The Family Doctor*, I arrived at medical school full of expectations. However, the inside of our dissection cadaver looked nothing like the hand-drawn depictions. Much of the learning was based on chemistry and physiology, and these invisible things were difficult to grasp. Facts and systemic interactions were added daily, each new dimension relying on the solidness of the previous layer. If your foundation had gaps in understanding, the fissure ran onwards and upwards, wider each year.

Also, you couldn't leave anything out. Even the most difficult things had to be mastered because you may encounter them in practice and 'I didn't learn that section' doesn't cut it with most patients. I had just slogged through one organ system when we would start with a new one. I felt like a dog tied to a racehorse.

But I worked hard, and I used my time wisely, and I got through.

Twenty-Four

There is a part of me that wishes that I would just get infected with Covid and get it over with, one way or the other. It seems inevitable that I will contract it sooner or later and my working theory is if I got it, and survived, I would feel bulletproof in the ED. I could get on and see patients without putting on a complete body cover and taking it off after each patient. Dressing up in all the layers and then removing them in a specific sequence is called 'donning and doffing' and we are all forced to attend video and live sessions to school us in the method. There is no point in wearing personal protective equipment if you don't do it correctly

Working with the airway of a positive patient is the highest risk for healthcare workers. Patients who have any kind of endoscope or ventilation shed the virus in massive clouds. It seems that anyone near them, including people who are transiently in the room, will definitely be exposed to the virus.

It makes sense to limit who is exposed. At the bigger hospitals like Baragwanath, there is a specialised team for the intubation of coronavirus positive patients. Two anaesthetists working together, in full personal protective equipment, respond to any unstable patient with Covid in the ED or the ward and will intubate them if needed. This team is quarantined between patients and individual members will stop working if they get any symptoms. One of my colleagues, who has two small children at home, is not expecting to see his family for more than a month. All of the registrars must take a turn at being on the team.

Today I read an article that postulates that people who have had the illness and recovered seem not to be developing immunity. After recovery from other viral infections, or a vaccination against a virus, antibodies should appear in the person's blood within about two weeks. This has been reliable with other viral infections like measles and mumps but with coronavirus, it seems that only 10 per cent of people who have had the infection develop antibodies to it. This means that, theoretically, one could get the infection again.

This is a blow to my theory that I should hurry up and get it over with. It would be frightful to fight the illness off, only to get it again.

I am pondering this disappointing news when I am called to high care for a resuscitation. When I arrive at the bedside, the patient is gasping, and the sister is saying a prayer.

'Lord Jesus Christ, I ask you to take mercy on her soul as we commit it to you in eternal heaven…' This is not a vote of confidence in my ability to resuscitate the patient and I hasten to interrupt her.

'Hang on a second. She's not dead yet. Start CPR.' The sister looks confused for a second and then snaps into action. The patient is a very old lady and I'm not sure if she is the one for active resuscitation. She is wearing a nappy and looks chronically ill. I ask whose patient it is and dial the admitting physician on my mobile.

I tell him that his patient, Mrs Cohen, has arrested in high care and ask if I should resuscitate her.

'Yes,' he replies with certainty. 'I am on my way.'

I give instructions for intravenous adrenaline and intubate the old lady. I am squeezing the bag when the physician arrives. He pulls back the curtain and stares at me for a moment and I am struck again by his unusually green eyes. He is a good-looking man and has a very kind heart, but he seems surprised that I am resuscitating Mrs Cohen.

It turns out that there are two Mrs. Cohens in high care. There is a young one with a very treatable pneumonia and this demented old lady, who is 96 and has been hanging about in Grim's waiting room for months.

'Oh,' I say with disappointment, 'Sorry.' The cardiac monitor is still showing me a flat line, so I cancel the resus and the physician goes to inform the family of her passing. The sister resumes her recommendation of the patient's soul to the powers that be and I turn to the basin to wash my hands and my equipment.

While I am standing with my back to the patient, lathering my hands and the laryngoscope with hot water, I hear the blip blip blip of a steady rhythm on the cardiac monitor behind me.

Granny is back.

It is well-documented that elderly people take longer to respond to resuscitation drugs than younger individuals. The look on the physician's face is priceless when he returns to the bedside. Granny has a pulse and a blood pressure and is breathing on her own.

'I did a good resuscitation, hey?' I tease him.

'No,' he replies, 'you did such a terrible job that she only recovered when you left her alone.' We laugh for a moment about this bizarre and unexpected turn of events, but he is left with the difficult decision about what to do next. He has already informed the family telephonically – they live overseas – and they are making arrangements to fly out to South Africa as soon as lockdown ends, but who knows when that will be. Chances are almost 100 per cent that granny's heart will stop again and that she will die within the next day. But what if she doesn't? What if they arrive to bury her and she is still holding on? We discuss the conundrum for a few minutes and conclude that he is going to have to call them back and tell them that a miracle has occurred.

Granny was dead, but 10 minutes after we stopped the resuscitation, she returned to life. Moments like this make me think of people who have been declared dead by an over-hasty doctor, only to have the corpse wake up in the mortuary.

Creepy thought, and the best-case scenario is to wake up in the fridge. While I am walking back to the ED, I think about some cultures who bury their dead with a little bell. Just in case. There are no patients waiting so I get busy on Google. Being buried alive is called vivisepulture and the fear of it, taphophobia. There is a YouTube video on what to do if you are buried alive. It has more than seven million views.

Unbelievable.

Twenty-Five

The ED staff is always bigger and better, and we have our own jargon and vocabulary of codes. Blocked coronary arteries, for instance, are 'widowmakers'. Calling events by a code helps to keep the general public from knowing what medical and security personnel are discussing. Instead of announcing 'dead person' over a public announcement, coded words are used. This is abbreviated to 'calling a code' as a general way to alert fellow medics that their assistance is required. A megacode is when you summon everyone, including porters and receptionists, to help, often in a disaster or multiple casualty situation.

We have all the war stories – the impossible resuscitations and the ridiculous things that patients have said or done.

I am working the night shift and, in the witching hour, a tall man wearing a soft neck brace comes in. He has shoulder-length curly hair and would be attractive if not for the jittery feel that surrounds him.

He is complaining of a whistling sound in his left nostril, a headache that has lasted for 10 years and the impulse to strangle himself. All of these are listed as the main complaint, but during the consultation he adds that he can only urinate if he leans to the left and he suspects that his neighbour broke into his flat yesterday and painted the walls with a sedative.

He is very agitated, especially considering that he has been inhaling sedative paint all night and I briefly consider trying to patent this idea as it could be a winner. He refuses to remove the cervical collar which he is using for self-protection from the strangling impulse. He thinks that the neck collar is causing the urinary retention, but I tell him that I doubt it. It is much more likely that all of his symptoms are coming from some kind of recreational drug that he is taking, and I direct my questions accordingly.

A friend who specialised in family medicine calls this 'setting the agenda for the consultation'. He books at least an hour with each patient and he wears a bow tie. I wear running shoes and scrubs and am lucky to get five minutes per patient.

The Collar Guy doesn't deny drug use and wants an injection to calm him down but he drove himself to the hospital so I cannot give him one. I suggest that I give him a few sleeping tablets to take at home. After protracted negotiation, all the time holding his left nostril closed to silence the whistling, he agrees to my plan.

I write out a prescription for sleeping tablets and give it to him. He goes to the pharmacy and is back within five minutes. I am in a cubicle with another patient, but he doesn't hesitate to open the door and ask me to lend him the money to fill the script.

It is not expensive, and it would be the quickest way to get rid of him, but lending money to patients is a bad idea. He assures me that he will repay me; it is just that he does not have his wallet with him tonight. He takes off his jeans to prove that he does not have a cent on him.

He is not wearing underpants.

'Too much information,' I joke with him and nudge him out of the cubicle before the other patient realises what is going on.

Later, the pharmacy manager shows me footage from the security cameras in the hospital foyer. Collar Guy presents the script to the pharmacy counter and the pharmacist processes it. She rings it up and he turns his pockets out looking for cash. He disappears from the video frame and the pharmacist puts the small white packet aside.

A few minutes pass and Collar Guy can be seen leopard

crawling into the image from the left. He looks around, his neck brace white against the grainy background. The pharmacist is not around, and he stands up, leans over the counter, snatches the bag and disappears.

Sadly for him, it is all on the video and the hospital takes the theft of medication very seriously, even if it is only a few tablets.

I wade my way through two more patients – one with a sore throat who didn't come in during the day because he wanted to avoid the non-existent queue and the next who thinks he has coronavirus because he ate a Chinese takeaway. I wonder where he got a takeaway during the lockdown and assure him that he does not need a swab as he has no symptoms at all.

Following close on his heels is a lady who needs painkillers for her fibromyalgia. I am flagging as it is four in the morning and I am wondering who would be awake at this time unless they had to be. She refers to 'My Fibro' with an unsettling edge of happy familiarity. It is like she is referring to a family pet rather than a debilitating set of symptoms.

It is quite a long word, fibromyalgia, but I have never heard patients abbreviating other diagnoses.

'I am spewing,' the next patient tells me. I have figured out that this means vomiting in the Indian community. I resignedly start to write out medication for nausea on her chart. I am tired by now and I want to go home

'And going out.'

'Going out?' I ask, confused. 'Going out where?'

'You know, going out.' She motions with her hand and I realise that she means that she has diarrhoea.

'Do you have any pain in your stomach?' I ask.

'No. But tell me, doctor,' the lady asks me, 'a cousin of ours has this poking pain right over here.' She prods my stomach. 'What could that be?'

'Well, it could be anything,' I reply. 'I would need to consult and examine him in order to give you my opinion.'

'Could it be cancer?'

'I suppose that it could be.'

'Oh, my goodness!' she exclaims. 'Did you hear that? ' She turns to her husband, 'He has cancer!'

'No, no,' I correct her. 'I didn't say that he has cancer. Just that it is on the list of possibilities. I would need to see him and do some tests.'

The lady eyes me beadily. I can see that she doesn't trust my diagnoses any longer. I am a turncoat.

What I am is an actress with a dark sense of humour. I use distraction and detachment to distance myself from the pain and panic of my everyday job, but there are still some patients who move me to tears and some situations where I cannot belittle the pathos and sadness that abound. I have enmeshed myself along the way into the persona of the grand old lady of the ED. It is inherent in the nature of a consultation that I am invisible and, after years of no one seeing me, I no longer see myself. In their moments of dark desperation, the patient needs a steady, confident hand on the helm. I have spent 30 years crafting both my skill and my performance in order to measure up. My wicked sense of the ridiculous gets me through the day and I have learned to silence my 'out-loud' voice; I render a sterling performance.

Twenty-Six

27 APRIL 2020

My partner Alida needs an operation on her knee. Because it is not a life-threatening condition, she has been waiting to see what happens with the pandemic. She is booked for Friday but, of course, she needs a Covid swab beforehand. She hobbled to the laboratory this morning to have the test and I am keeping an eye on the lab App for her result.

I have a sneaky suspicion that it is going to be positive.

She knows the risk of living with a front-line worker and neither of us has been ill, but we haven't been feeling fantastic over the past two weeks. A vague malaise, slight shortness of breath and fatigue. It could all be psychological, of course.

I am working the late shift today, which is enough to make anyone feel off-colour. A sheepish-looking man is outside, refusing to tell the triage nurse why he wants to see the doctor. It is late and I am tired; I'm not up for an argument so I take the file from the clerk and call the patient through.

He tells me a long and detailed story about how he lost his keys and had to break into his own house. He climbed through the pantry window and, when he was halfway through, his foot slipped. He had been straddling the shelf beneath the window and a bottle of tomato sauce had accidentally slipped into his anus.

Without blinking, I process this story and then ask the obvious question.

'Why were you naked?'

129

An awkward moment of silence and then a deep flush spread up his neck. I must try very hard to keep my face expressionless. I raise my hand to rub my nose and disguise a smile, even though I am wearing a mask.

There is no way other than surgery to recover that tomato sauce bottle. And herein lies the rub – because this seemingly dowdy, middle-aged man was not at home with his wife when the accident occurred.

How are we going to explain the abdominal surgery to his wife and family without actually telling a lie? Patient confidentiality is vital, but there are forms to fill in and we need to get medical aid authorisation. We can't write a fake diagnosis and the patient does not have enough cash to pay privately. As is the habit of the ED doctor, I pass this quandary on to the admitting surgeon, who thinks the situation is hysterically funny. At least I have brightened up his evening.

Stories abound in the ED about foreign bodies in the vagina and rectum. Sex toys, condoms, tampons, various tools and implements. My personal favorite was reported in a British journal. A man had come in with abdominal pain and an X-ray revealed a tin can in his descending colon. Initially he had no knowledge of how it got there, but later admitted that he had inserted it per rectum. He had to go to the theatre for a laparotomy to get it out. The surgeon proudly placed the recovered tin of baked beans on the draped tray. The scrub nurse looked on, puzzled. 'Cor,' she said, 'fancy eatin' them in the tin!'

Needless to say, the attending surgeon did not correct her perception of how the intact tin had ended up in the patient's colon.

I have a vague sense of disquiet and I realise it is because I am still waiting for the swab result. I open the App and type in my partner's identity number. The result is ready. I click on the link and there it is.

Her SARS CoV2 test is positive.

My heart sinks. I suspected it, but to see the result in black and white is deeply alarming. The results are in capitals and surrounded by asterisks, as if the phone is shouting at me. I have almost finished my shift and decide to discuss it in person when I get home.

At first she thinks that I am playing a prank on her. I have a wicked sense of humour but I never joke about people's health. I assure her that I am being serious and show her the result on my phone. A heavy silence ensues.

'So, what does that mean?' she asks eventually.

'It means I must have given it to you.' I tell her. 'You have been at home on crutches for five weeks. Where else would you have contracted it? I have been working with sick patients for months.'

'I wish I hadn't taken the test,' she tells me ruefully.

It is going to play havoc with my life, but I tell her that I am glad that she tested before she had the procedure. Evidence shows that people have a more than ten-fold increase in complications if they have surgery when they are Covid positive. I think that this is because of the clotting abnormalities that the virus causes.

But, of course, I cannot be sure of anything when it comes to coronavirus.

What I am sure of is that I have to tell the ED and I will be quarantined until I have two negative results over a period of at least a week.

I call in first thing and set the cat amongst the pigeons. I am the first definite link that many people have had, and I know that alarm will ripple through the hospital. People that I passed in the corridor over the past 10 days will be rushing to test and I must come in immediately for a swab.

They are waiting for me in the parking lot. Colleagues that I have worked with for more than 20 years are dressed in space suits and beckon me into a container, like flight officials direct a Boeing. They are lacking the little orange table tennis bats, but otherwise I can almost hear their fear like the relentless roar of turbine engines.

I somehow know that my test will be negative, and it is. The test is a PCR, or polymerase chain reaction, which looks for the virus itself. There are no tests for antibodies available yet in South Africa.

I have a whole week to work on the farm. Seven days away from work is unheard of for me and, despite my uneasy heart, I decide to make the best of them. I set off to fix fences and trim back trees, play the cello and make lemon–almond tart.

We are visited by the Department of Health the day after the test results come out and I am surprised by how helpful the nurses are. Mostly they want to play with the greyhounds, but they also take a thorough look around the farmhouse to ensure that we are able to isolate properly. Alida has to take her temperature every day and message it to the nurse. I also check her temperature if she looks flushed or blows her nose. Sometimes I even check it while she is sleeping. But both of us sail along with no symptoms, except for a strange taste on my tongue and some fatigue.

To my amazement, my week in isolation passes very quickly and seven days later I am back in the container getting a swab.

Negative again. If I wear protective equipment I can go back to work.

I am genuinely surprised at how happy I am to walk through those double doors again.

Twenty-Seven

The ED is still deserted. Our shifts have been cut and the staff is thin on the ground. I feel unnaturally tired today and it is all that I can do to stay awake. Not even a patient with a stabbed abdomen piques my interest. I put up a drip, send him for a scan and call the surgeon. There is a loop of bowel hanging out of the wound, but the patient is adamant that he doesn't need surgery. His wife stabbed him, so I guess he is an indirect victim of the lockdown.

'Don't cut me,' he keeps repeating. I want to tell him it's too late for that mantra, but it feels like too much effort to engage. Maybe I am coming down with Covid.

The nurse from triage comes through to ask my opinion. Giving my opinion is what I do for a living and it tries my nerves when patients attempt to avoid paying a consultation fee by asking the nurse to enquire on their behalf, without opening a file. I cannot give an opinion without getting the whole story, which is essentially a consultation. I usually manage to insist that the patient opens a file before I give my opinion but the nurse is one of my favourites and she looks stressed, so I hear her out.

There is a couple outside with a two-year-old girl. They tell the nurse that they came home from the shops to find their 14-year-old son on top of their little girl. Both children were naked, and the boy had an erection. They want the doctor to check whether 'anything happened.' I stare at the nurse.

Something certainly happened. The definition of sexual abuse does not require penetration. And this involves a minor and so we must report it to the police.

We go out into the waiting room together. The child is playing with crayons at the table in the corner. I ask the nurse to watch her while I take the parents into the side ward to discuss it with them.

'Any sexual contact, including just rubbing or groping, constitutes sexual assault. It means that we will have to report it to the police and open a case against your son. We will need to examine your little girl and check that there is no obvious injury, and she cannot go home into the same house as the perpetrator. Do you have family that your son or daughter can stay with?'

The parents look both confused and alarmed. 'Can't we just send him to counselling?' they ask hopefully. 'If she isn't injured or anything…' the mother trails off half-heartedly. 'Maybe he was just fooling around.'

I think back to myself at 14. I most certainly would have known that what I was doing was wrong. And then there is the issue of the age of the victim. Surely molesting any two-year-old doesn't feel like the right thing to do, even if she is not your sister? I am not sure how sexuality enters this picture at all.

The mother then tells me that she beat the boy with a sjambok. Great. Now there are two cases to be opened.

To my amazement, our local police station answers on the first ring and has the mobile number for child protection services. Even more amazing, the child protection officer answers his mobile and arrives in the ED 10 minutes later. Miracles never cease.

I am distracted from the family consultation by a young woman throwing her phone at her mother in the waiting room. There is a lot of shouting and I am relieved that there are only paper cups at the water cooler as one goes flying through the open window. A smoker outside the ED looks in with interest as the drama unfolds. When I get the young lady alone in one of the rooms, she is well-mannered and tearful. The furious banshee has dissipated, and I ask her what made her so angry.

She has quite a tale to tell. When she was six years old her mother booked them on an overseas trip. They were stopped at the airport because her daughter's pretty unicorn backpack had layers of narcotics sewn into the seams. Mom claimed innocence and alleged that someone had swapped her daughter's luggage, but the police were having none of it. The mother was arrested and the little girl, after a bewildering swirl of activity, was sent to be cared for by her aunt. Five years later her aunt passed away from acute leukemia and the young lady became flotsam in the foster system until she turned 18.

Now her mother is out of jail. She is unemployed and is trying to foster a relationship with her estranged daughter. Mom is still using drugs and manipulating everything around her and this young lady has had enough. She is furious with her mother, the system and the world and is, in my opinion, at real risk of harming herself or someone else. If there ever was a patient deserving of help, it is she. But they have no medical aid and no cash and counselling is a scarce commodity in the state sector. Psychiatric beds are almost impossible to find and are reserved for properly psychotic patients rather than this young lady, who would benefit from years of psychotherapy. In any case, she is not interested in being admitted anywhere.

I chat to her for a while, sounding out whether there is any avenue like a church that she would be comfortable with for counselling. As I suspected, mainstream society has not been kind to her, and she is as wary as a fox. I have a brainwave and remember that the university takes on pro deo cases for the Masters students in clinical psychology to cut their therapeutic teeth on. Although she is going to be a complicated case, the students are well supervised, and I think it could work.

I set about arranging it. Once we are out of stage five of the lockdown, I can get her an appointment.

Twenty-Eight

Lockdown is lifted from stage five to stage four today. Excitement abounds. We are allowed to go outside to exercise, but only from 6 to 9 in the mornings. We must move about singly and not in groups. We must still stay home from work unless we are an essential service but some of the other rules are relaxed. We still cannot buy alcohol and books. In an about-turn, the government says that cigarettes will not be for sale. This has outraged the smoking public, many of whom have been rationing themselves with the first of May as their goal.

For the first time since the lockdown, the public is doubting the government's wisdom. Many people cannot work, and businesses will close. The knock-on effect will be enormous.

Stage four does not make much difference to my lifestyle. I still go to work every day, but my hours are slightly shorter. I earn less but I spend less.

The South African public has been groomed into unwilling obedience with the terminology of stages. We already understand that staging is associated with deprivation as the national power utility uses staging to inform us of when the grid is under pressure and electricity will be rationed. And we understand that, whether the staging is for electricity production or Covid control, it is for our own good.

That does not make us happy with the situation, but it helps with compliance.

Since the corona outbreak I have stopped making tea or instant soup in the ED because all the crockery feels contaminated. Seven in the morning would usually see me at my post, cup steaming, waiting for patients. Now I just sit on my chair and wipe everything in sight with alcohol swabs.

Who would have thought that a time would come when my hands see more alcohol than my lips?

The red phone rings as I am wiping it. It startles me, chirping under my hand, and I clean the handset before speaking into it. Paramedics are bringing a 50-year-old man who collapsed with chest pain while running. They tell me that his ECG is abnormal. I alert the cardiologist and tell him that I will call him once I have assessed the patient.

Half an hour goes by and there is no sign of the patient. Perhaps they took him to a different hospital. Perhaps he died. Perhaps, hopefully, he will only arrive after the end of my shift.

No such luck. The doorbell chimes almost an hour after the phone call. The paramedics have dripped and intubated the patient and they are doing CPR. The paramedic in charge is trying to look calm.

'This is a 50-year-old male patient who complained to his wife of chest pain while running. The ECG showed a myocardial infarction but unfortunately he went into cardiac arrest immediately upon our arrival.' He shows me the initial ECG. Definitely a heart attack with the classic tombstone appearance of the ST segments. Between the S and the T waves, the tracing on a normal ECG should return to the baseline in a directly downward trajectory. In the typical heart attack, this segment of the ECG makes an upright hump, like the profile of a tombstone against the sky.

No need to hunt for Hs and Ts for this arrest.

'We started CPR at the roadside. He was initially in ventricular fibrillation and we shocked him four times and gave eight doses of adrenaline intravenously. We also gave amiodarone while he was fibrillating. The rhythm changed to asystole about 10 minutes ago. We then gave more adrenaline and three amps of atropine intravenously. We have had no return of spontaneous circulation.'

I stare at the team. Essentially, they are telling me that the patient dropped dead in front of them an hour ago and he is still dead. They have followed the protocol and done everything that there is to do. His heart was initially quivering, or fibrillating, which they tried to shock, to no avail, and now it has stopped completely.

'Ok so you have done everything, and this is an unsuccessful resuscitation.' I summarise. I have to ask the obvious. 'So why did you bring him to the ED and not just declare him dead at the scene?'

The paramedic looks embarrassed and shrugs. 'His family was with him.'

'No way,' I think. The paramedic is telling me that they brought a dead patient to ED so that I can tell his family that he is dead. To make matters worse, he is a private patient. So, I will have to call his family in, tell them that he is dead, and then ask them for money.

Needless to say, this ruins my day. I try not to have people die in the ED. Aside from making me feel like a bad doctor, it generates an enormous amount of paperwork.

Bad news travels fast and soon we are swamped with family and friends of the deceased runner. They are weeping and wailing, and one is even lying on the floor, comatose with grief. The dead body takes an examination cubicle out of commission, the waiting room is overflowing, and everyone is edgy and unsettled.

Each new patient who comes through has heard that we had a death in the unit and every single one asks if it was coronavirus. Under normal circumstances we would not discuss another patient's diagnosis but today I just say that I don't think it is causally related. It seems only fair to allay their fears if I can. I do think that corona may have played a role as he probably hadn't done any exercise during the lockdown and he certainly hadn't been holding back on eating snacks. There is also evidence that corona increases clotting and that even patients with no respiratory symptoms can have an increased risk of heart attacks and strokes. I arrange a swab of the dead man's throat and then get caught up in administration because post-mortems are not being done during the lockdown.

I am on my motorbike today and I can't wait to get out of here. I have headphones in my helmet, and I select Dire Straits for the drive home. Leathers on, a throaty gurgle and I'm gone. Slow throbbing through the suburbs, but on the open road I twist the throttle and the late summer night blasts by. The tarmac is a black ribbon stretching through the dark fields to meet a sky full of stars. Mark Knopfler is a genius on the strings, drowning out the roar of the steel and chrome. The wind buffets my chest and blows the day's images out of my head.

Slower now on the dirt, the road is a farm track with twin ruts and a grassy hump in the middle. The last heads of summer seed nod to me as I pass in the eerie light. The bike is heavy and the back tyre weaves in the thick red sand. I stop to push the farm gate open and stand for a moment, a lone figure in the night. The engine ticks and gurgles, burning from the ride.

The snoopies are waiting, bounding down the driveway, their coats gleaming in the wash of the headlight.

Alida is reading in the kitchen, the enamel kettle singing on the wood stove. The farmhouse is warm, but we dress the greyhounds in light jackets for bedtime. It is pointless to cover them before I come home as they will trail blankets and jackets down the driveway to greet me.

I pour us both a whiskey and lock the world out. I need news of the day's activities on the farm and to change gear before I can sleep.

I am glad to be home.

Twenty-Nine

It is a lovely crisp autumn morning and I take the snoopies for a walk before work. They don't know anything about the pandemic, and I wonder if they notice that the world is quieter without the traffic and bustle. They bound through the fields as only greyhounds can, their coats gleaming in the morning sun. They are such perfect athletes; I watch them affectionately and wish that they would never get old.

I can't put my finger on the flimsy border between quietness and depression. Our world is forever changed, as I imagine it was for our parents during wartime. I can think of a few positive things that we can glean from this difficult time. Life has taken on a different pace and some of us who were always rushing past each other are starting to change our ways. I, certainly, had lost touch with silence and taking my time and, even with social distancing, I have had more meaningful interactions with friends and family over the past few weeks.

But I still can't shake off this inexorable sadness and caution that is sitting like a stone in my heart. It is shapeless but heavy and it feels like there is a filter between the world and the sun, screening a little of the brightness out.

I try to push the queue in the ED, hoping that action will shake off the melancholia. I am working with an infamously slow junior doctor today. She writes about three pages of notes on every patient, documenting the most bizarre things that, in my opinion, have nothing to do with the presenting complaint.

Everyone must learn sometime, and slow doctors are much better to work with than lazy ones. Junior doctors are completely at the mercy of their seniors and not only are lazy doctors no help in managing the tsunami of patients, but they can actively obstruct patient care.

There is also the hope, in the back of my mind, that a slow doctor will speed up when they get more experience. These days I might be too quick with the patients, but I can't recall ever taking as long in a consultation as she does. Even more frustratingly, she comes and presents the endless history and examination to me after each patient and asks me what to do next.

It is too tedious for speech.

I knew a registrar who took almost two hours to do his first Caesaraen section. Given that an experienced gynae can do a Caesar in 15 minutes skin to skin – meaning from the first cut to last stitch – this was painstakingly slow. The anaesthetist was resting his head on the ventilator and staring at the floor when he realised, to his horror, that the patient was booked for a sterilisation as part of the same procedure.

'Don't worry about the steri, mate,' he said dryly to the registrar. 'The patient will be menopausal by the time you finish.'

Two years later, that registrar had such smooth hands that he was doing 20 Caesars a night and not breaking a sweat.

Laziness is much more difficult to rectify.

When I was a houseman on surgical rotation, I had a painfully lazy and arrogant registrar. He fancied himself as a lady's man and was always chatting on the phone or sending text messages. I never saw him put a hand on a patient. He would lurk at the back of the ward round, out of sight for questions and instructions. On intake he would go straight to his room and tell his juniors that he needed to study and that we should not call him unless absolutely necessary.

Even as a student I hated night shift. It wasn't exciting; it was tiring and lonely and full of strange people. On a month-end Saturday night a man came in with a gunshot wound to his neck. He was very drunk and had been shot by his brother-in-law during an argument. I can't imagine taking such rash action, especially against a member of my family, but he didn't seem to think it too unusual.

There were two round holes on the right side of his neck and the edges of the one wound were burned black with gunpowder. It seemed the bullet had travelled through him and we confirmed on a portable X-ray that it was not still inside. The man's blood pressure and pulse were stable. Nevertheless, there are a lot of very important structures in the neck and I felt that he should be admitted for observation and further tests. As usual, the registrar was hiding in his room, but I let him know about the case.

The next morning the patient was sitting up in his bed in the ward and no further tests had been done. The consultant was outraged – clearly the registrar had not seen the patient at all; he was still wearing his street clothes and the two blood-stained dressings from the ED. The consultant spoke sternly to the registrar and told him that he had better make sure the wound was thoroughly investigated and debrided by the end of the day.

The registrar lazily filled in a request for a CT angiogram and gave it to me to organise. After the round, he told me that he was not prepared to wait for the patient to come back from the CT and I must check the result and then debride the wound when the patient got back to the ward. I looked at him with alarm.

'I don't know how to debride a wound.' My confession earned me a scathing look.

'You just give local anaesthetic and cut off any dead or black tissue around the edge. Then you stitch the raw edges together.'

It sounded easy, so I agreed to do it.

Snip, snip, I trimmed the edge of the wound, my nose inches from the patient. On about the fourth snip, I cut a small artery. Blood squirted onto my cheek.

'Oops.' A word that you don't want to hear during a procedure.

I put some pressure on it. The patient squirmed.

'Sorry.' I said. It kept bleeding briskly. Damn. Sunday afternoon and there were no other doctors in the unit. I should never have agreed to do this. There is a limit to how much pressure you can put on a person's neck without killing them. I tried to grasp the bleeding vessel with a little clamp called a mosquito. It pinched the patient's skin and he yelped.

'Sorry.' I said again.

It kept bleeding. I put on another mosquito, and another until there was a whole nest of them sticking up from his neck. The patient had slithered as far away from me as he could and was covering his eyes with his blood-stained T-shirt. The mosquitos jangled and quivered against each other, but the bleeding had stopped. My heart was hammering, and my shirt was drenched with sweat. I was not sure which of the mosquitos had done the trick, so I tied a suture around the base of all of them and knotted it tight. Then I took them off, one by one. I was afraid to even breathe on the patient. I felt like I had aged about 20 years in 10 minutes.

I stood and stared at the wound for a full five minutes. It looked awful, the skin puckered into an ugly heap, but it had stopped bleeding and I was not going to touch it again. I stuck on a dressing and told the patient not to make any sudden movements.

On the Monday morning grand round, the consultant peeled off the dressing. He gasped in horror and turned on the registrar.

'What on earth is this?'

The registrar blushed and stammered, but there was no escape; his laziness and negligence were apparent and clear to all. I felt vindicated.

Thirty

hings are busier now that we are at level four of lockdown. People are falling off their bicycles again on a Sunday morning. Cyclists have always kept the ED in business over the weekends and my first customer today hit the ground harder than most. The paramedics tell me that he was travelling at about 60 kilometres per hour when he encountered an unseen speed bump. Strangely, he is wearing work clothes, rather than traditional cycling gear, and he was not wearing a helmet. The right side of his face took the brunt of the fall. His ear is hanging from his scalp by a thread of skin and his cheek gapes open. More concerning, he is soundly unconscious. This means I cannot get any other information from him as regards other injuries, so I send him down for a pan-scan.

In years gone by, X-rays were the standard investigation for trauma. But studies show that plain X-rays can miss up to half of the possible life-threatening injuries, even if reported by a radiologist. Current guidelines tell us that, if there is any suspicion of serious injury, we must do a CT scan. A pan-scan is essentially a scan of the whole core of the patient – head to pelvis.

A sister accompanies the patient to the scanner, and I hear nothing for half an hour. They should be back by now and I go downstairs to find out what is happening. I walk first to the CT room and peer through the porthole. The room is deserted. I double back to the waiting room and eventually find my cyclist lying unattended in the corner of the X-ray department. He is covered with a blanket, snoring and still immobilised on the stretcher. The monitoring machines are attached but there is no staff in sight, despite my ordering the scan as urgent almost an hour ago. I stomp around until I find the radiographer and ask her what is going on. She can tell I am irritated despite my face being concealed behind a mask and she tells me sulkily that she was X-raying other patients. I remind her that this scan is urgent and tell her to hurry up.

I feel her glaring at my departing back. Too bad. The cyclist is unconscious and so I am his only advocate.

I am justified in requesting the scan as the cyclist has a small bleed in his brain as well as a broken neck, multiple broken ribs and a ruptured spleen. The amputated ear is the least of his worries.

I dispatch him to the Milpark trauma unit and slog on with the next patient.

There is nothing easy in the ED today. Everyone needs blood tests or X-rays or stitches, so I am pleased to see that the next consultation is for a tick bite. It should be quick and easy. The patient is a 10-year-old boy and his whole family traipse into the cubicle and gather around as his mother pulls down his sock. She reveals the tick, which is still attached. I pluck it off and flush it down the drain. They stare at me in horror.

'You pulled it off!'

'Yes, of course. It can't stay there.'

'But what if you left the head inside?'

I explain away this myth – that ticks somehow become detached from their heads when you pull them off and that the imbedded head grows another body – and tell them to keep an eye on the bite to make sure an eschar does not develop. I google eschar on my phone and show them what it looks like: A red area with a grey to black centre, which, together with swollen, tender glands, a headache and fever will signal the start of tick bite fever. The incubation is usually 10 days exactly. Blood tests are unreliable; the diagnosis relies on history and identification of the eschar.

In my experience, patients who develop tick bite fever seldom find the tick attached. Perhaps because the tick is sick with Rickettsial disease itself and so it is weak and falls off before it is discovered. This is just a theory of mine, formulated over the years. Like the association between thumb rings and borderline personality disorder and the possibility that people with tattoos are more afraid of needles than the general population. It's just a hunch, really.

There is a lot of screaming going on in the waiting room. A mother comes through, clutching a baby to her chest. Her shirt is splattered with blood. She is screaming, the baby is screaming, and an older lady – probably granny – is also screaming. There is a small child in tow, and they are all screaming at each other and screaming at the staff. Soon they are screaming at me.

'I wanna go home!' The little girl wails.

'So do I!' I want to shout. The whole situation looks pretty frightful but once we clean the blood off, we find it is only a laceration to the baby's ear. Their excitable puppy had bitten her by mistake.

I give the baby some Valeron drops for pain and they all settle down a bit. The laceration is small but deep – the top of her ear is divided in half vertically and will need to be lined up precisely. In an adult it would be difficult to fix in the ED but in a small baby it is pretty much impossible.

I explain to the mom that we need to admit the baby for the plastic surgeon and have the ear fixed under sedation. Granny goes out to open the file and the mom confides in me that they are not on medical aid. Her husband lost his job at the beginning of lockdown and so their cover has lapsed. I give her an estimate of price and she says there is no way that they can afford it. I suggest we send them to a government hospital, but she is not interested.

'Can't we just put a dressing on it?'

'No,' I reply. 'We won't get a good result. The top part of her ear is split in half and it won't knit together if we don't oppose the edges of the wound accurately. If we end up with a step or notch in the top of her ear, it will be very noticeable.'

'My mother's coming back in a minute,' she tells me urgently. 'You can't tell her about the medical aid. She hates my husband already – this will be the last straw.'

As I open my mouth to answer, granny dashes back into the cubicle.

'I need your medical aid card, darling, to open the file.'

'The doctor says we don't need to bother, Mom. It just needs a dressing.'

I am speechless for a second.

'No, well, we still need a file for the ED consult,' I say quickly.

This is a first for me. Patients often request a plastic surgeon before I even look at the wound. A few years ago, a 90-year-old man came in with a tiny laceration on the bridge of his nose. He had been cut with a shard of glass from a broken light bulb. The man was no oil painting and the laceration was barely visible on his huge beak amongst the liver spots and sun damage. He asked to be referred to a plastic surgeon; I laughed and said 'yes, sure'. The temperature in the room dropped about 10 degrees.

'Oh,' I corrected myself, 'you're actually serious.'

Today, I am not about to attempt to fix this baby's ear, regardless of the family dynamics. I put a saline dressing over it with a bandage around the baby's head.

'This dressing is just temporary; she will need to have her ear fixed by a plastic surgeon,' I tell the whole family solemnly. I make no mention of the cost and their lack of medical aid. I give them a referral letter and a map to the local government hospital. Granny looks confused as they make their way back to reception. I think the crisis is averted until I hear the receptionist telling them, loudly, that the consultation fee will have to be settled in cash as their medical aid is suspended.

I feel sorry for the whole family and the absent, retrenched husband.

Thirty-One

Alcohol does not mix well with an open flame. I have lost count of the burns on fingers and toes that I have seen from men throwing volatile liquids on a fire in order to 'get it going'. It is usually petrol rather than whiskey and my current patient's right ear was also in the line of fire, so to speak. It has been burned beyond recognition because he turned his face to the left in an attempt to avoid the approaching fireball.

It is strange how injuries seem to come in clusters. This is the third injured ear I have seen today. All on the right-hand side.

As to why I have never seen a woman with this type of injury, I suppose that men are more often tasked with starting the fire. Maybe they know more about flammable liquids. Perhaps they are less risk averse.

The last patient that I saw with such a severely burned ear was trying to cut a steel barrel in half with an angle grinder. Sadly for him, the barrel had previously been used to store aviation fuel and was still full of fumes. The sparks from the steel grinder ignited a massive explosion that saw Mr Handyman in the prolonged care of a plastic surgeon for multiple skin grafts.

My patient today has ruined the family braai by throwing acetone on the smouldering coals and needs to be admitted as more than 20 per cent of his body surface has been burned. The percentage is worked out using what's called the Rule of Nines, a system of scoring each limb as 9 per cent and a more complicated ratio for the head and body.

First aid instructors love to quiz their students about the Rule of Nines. I can't really see the point of the calculation for a first aider, especially as the extent of the burn cannot be assessed in the first few minutes, but I know that the trauma surgeon will ask, so I work it out as roughly 30 per cent. Mr Fireball will need antibiotics, fluids and strong painkillers. Luckily for us both, he has no inhalation burns. I put on dressings, arrange the admission and write up the medication.

I sit on the shirking wall and google the gender distribution of arsonists. I see that female arsonists have a very specific psychiatric profile, but I don't get to read further as a sister comes to tell me that there is a patient waiting.

Throwing petrol on a fire may constitute stupidity rather than arson, I think, as I slip in through the double doors. The pandemic has made me an expert at getting through doorways without touching the handles.

The patient-in-waiting is an elderly woman with a dog bite on her hand. She is upset and I ask her what happened. The tears well up and flow down her cheeks.

'My little dog.' She falters and stops. 'A dog in the park attacked my little dog. I was trying to save her, and I got bitten.'

'Oh no,' I say. 'Is your dog OK?' She shakes her head and cannot speak. Her sorrow resonates with the dull depression loitering in my heart. What a terrible thing to happen. She is so sad and her little dog is gone. I feel foolish but my heart is breaking for her. I am suddenly overwhelmed and self-conscious; I can feel the sister staring at me, but I am helpless to stop my own tears. I wipe them silently away and stare down at the file until I can get a grip on myself.

I know that for this lady the world will never be the same. I dread her loneliness and the self-recrimination to come. I am sure the trauma of today will overshadow all of the good years and the loyal companionship that she had. I want to ask her the little dog's name, but I also cannot speak.

I know that when she finds her voice she will keep saying 'if only'. When she wakes alone in her flat, listening for the click of claws or feeling for the slumbering weight by her feet, she will go over and over the horrific event in her mind.

'If only' may be the two most tragic words in the English language.

Thirty-Two

The general feeling of discontent is growing. Many people think that the lockdown was instrumental in giving the healthcare profession time to prepare for the pandemic. Flattening the curve was about spacing out the cases and giving us all time to have our equipment and protocols ready.
We are now as ready as we are ever going to be.

People are hungry and restless. At least the ED is a bit busier so we may get paid at month end. But our economy is already fragile, and I am genuinely worried about the future.

So far it seems that there may be a different strain of the virus in the Western Cape than that which we have in Gauteng. The pandemic is seeing a much higher percentage of deaths there.

A fretful father brings his son to the ED. The boy is about five and he fell off a jungle gym. He had no loss of consciousness and no neurological symptoms but there is a laceration on his forehead which is gaping, and he will need stitches.

I examine the boy and find that the edges of the cut come together quite well. I am confident that I can do a good job stitching it and we can do it now under local anaesthetic. Most of the laceration is covered by his hair anyway. Alternatively, they can go to a plastic surgeon but he will only fix the wound tomorrow in the theatre as the child ate a burger on his way to the hospital. Unless surgery is super urgent, patients must be fasting before being anaesthetised. If there is food in the stomach, there is the risk of it being regurgitated and inhaled and an aspiration pneumonia is a disastrous complication. If the patient must be operated on immediately, the anaesthetist can do what is called a crash induction, which means that they move really quickly through the steps of putting the patient to sleep, and try to hold the airway shut until the very last moment when the tube is introduced. No one is going to suggest emergency surgery for this laceration and it will make no cosmetic difference if it is fixed today or tomorrow. The boy would also need to be swabbed for Covid before being allowed into the theatre.

'Just fix it here,' Dad says. He is not too worried about scarring and does not want to expose his son to the germs in the hospital. I tell him that I think that he is making the right decision.

The boy was hoping he wouldn't need stitches and he is rigid with fear.

'Hiya,' I say, addressing him directly. 'What's your name?' I could look on the file but I have certain rules of engagement.

'Jake.' His voice is tremulous, and his huge eyes track my every move.

'Jake!' I say. 'I have a greyhound called Jake.'

'Really?' His interest is evident, so I show him a photograph on my mobile phone. Jake is a handsome fellow and, as luck would have it, I recently stitched a huge laceration on his haunch. Greyhounds have too much gas and no brakes; they are also lean and muscular and their skin tears like paper. I compare the cuts on the two Jakes and soon we are chatting away. He lies still while I clean the wound and slowly give some local anaesthetic. As I pick up the needle-holder to start suturing, the curtain is ripped open.

'What do you think you are doing?' I nearly jump out of my skin and turn to see an older woman with shocking red hair standing behind me. Her hands are on her hips and her painted lips downturned like a bloody gash.

'I have been the matron of the General Hospital for 35 years,' she bellows. 'My grandson needs to see a plastic surgeon. I have sent the picture of the wound to the head of surgery and he says it is an extremely severe cut that even he could not repair!'

I blink. I don't want to point out that anyone who still calls it the General Hospital is way out of touch; that I have never seen a matron, retired or not, with that colour hair and that any general surgeon that cannot fix such a small laceration must be a poor surgeon indeed.

'We did discuss the option of a plastic surgeon,' I say mildly, 'and we decided to go ahead and fix it here. Most of the laceration is in the hairline and I'm sure that I'll get a good result.'

'Under no circumstances.' I can see that she is serious.

'But I've already given him local.' I say lamely.

'Doesn't matter. I will pay for it.'

'Payment is not the issue,' I say, but I can see that I am going to lose this battle. Jake starts to cry.

'Please just fix it,' he implores.

I look appealingly at his father, but he gives me a thousand-yard stare. It seems that everyone, including myself, is under the matron's domination. I put a dressing over the wound.

'Sorry, Jake,' I say. I cannot not stitch him without his parent's consent.

Thirty-Three

I am feeling bleak. Coronavirus is wearing me down and greedy Grim has the upper hand today. He is taking all the nice people or perhaps the imminent crossing over brings out the best in people.

Tonight, I have an elderly man who came by ambulance. It is his 80th birthday and he is not feeling well but is non-specific about what, exactly, is wrong with him. For the past week he has had a loss of appetite, general lethargy and dark-coloured urine. No chest pain, no cough, no fever. On initial examination I think he looks dehydrated and his blood pressure is low but there isn't much else to find.

The sister at the retirement village tested his urine and checked his blood pressure yesterday. She told him to drink lots of fluid and to go to the hospital if he doesn't feel better. He feels worse today, so here he is.

I put up a drip, pull blood and ask the sister to do an ECG and a urine sample. Of course, we must swab him for Covid, but that result will only come back tomorrow.

The ECG shows changes that are borderline abnormal, but the blood test results are off the charts. Values that should be less than five are in the thousands and I speak to the cardiologist. He asks for a diagnosis and I tell him that I am not sure. It is possible that he had a heart attack a week ago, with no symptoms at the time, but this seems unlikely. The cardiologist postulates that he may have an infection and he suggests that I speak to the physician.

The physician listens to my story and suggests that I speak to the cardiologist.

Eventually, between the two of them, they accept the patient and I admit him to the ICU.

He waves to me as he gets wheeled out, his family following along, but 10 minutes later the Code Blue bell rings. There is an emergency in ICU, and I see that the cardiologist is calling me at the same time on my mobile. I set off at speed, answering my phone as I depart the ED. My patient has crashed.

Damn.

I race along the corridor, past the worried family that just left the ED, and into the ICU. The cardiologist and the physician are doing CPR. I take over chest compressions and the cardiologist is freed up to do a sonar of his heart. When he is ready, we stop compressions and he puts the probe on the patient's chest.

We see that the patient has a ruptured mitral valve. This valve lies on the left side of the heart between the top and bottom chambers and so, every time his heart contracts, it sends half of the blood backwards to his lungs instead of forwards to his body.

There is nothing to be done and we declare him dead a few minutes later. Neither the cardiologist nor the physician have met the family, so I suppose that I must go and give them the news.

I brace myself for the grief. At least he made 80 in pretty good shape and the end was swift. What more can we ask for? He had a good innings, as my mother would say. It is much harder to break bad news about babies and children. I have watched mothers clutching their dead babies for hours and widows kissing the ice-cold lips of a body that was the vessel of the soul they loved.

It seems to me that grief is initially overwhelming, but over time the sadness, the longing and the absence become background music. Sometimes, it drowns everything out, and sometimes, it's only audible when you sit quietly and listen.

Wow, what an interesting case, my colleagues say later. Why

would his mitral valve rupture? Did he have infective endocarditis? Was it a weakness caused by a silent heart attack? Everyone is fascinated by the mystery but I just find it depressing.

It feels like nothing we did had any effect on the trajectory of events. Moments like this make you doubt yourself to the core.

Working in the ED requires nerves of steel to make it through. At the end of the day, you, and your patients, will be lucky to get out of there alive. Once you lose your nerve, you are toast.

Medicine can be a spiteful lover, building you up one moment to slap you down the next. When things go well, you are admired and respected. But one wrong move, one missed diagnosis and all is lost.

I am deeply ambivalent about my job – it is utterly exhausting but exhilarating too. I think of the ED as a jungle, full of traps. You can't see them, of course, because traps are inherently invisible. You may be moving along, oblivious, when suddenly you see that the fronds are moving. It's an ambush. You move from complacency to blind panic in a matter of seconds. A car pulls up at the door with a drowned child or a cardiac arrest and you are suddenly in the middle of a devastating storm.

I want to sit sulkily on the shirking wall until the end of my shift but one of the paramedics intercepts me. He needs to learn to suture. He has a job lined up on an oil rig and stitching basic wounds is one of the core competencies. His ability to do this must be assessed and signed off by a registered medical practitioner.

This assumes that all registered medical practitioners know how to suture. No–one ever taught me how to stitch – it was something that I just kind of picked up along the way during my time in The Pit at Baragwanath Hospital.

Watch one, do one, teach one.

I enjoy teaching so, if the patient is happy and the ED is not too busy, I have no problem helping him out.

We are like surfers waiting for a wave as we watch the patients come through the doors. I have an image of the ocean at dawn, sitting on our boards beyond the breakers and riding the swells. He is eager to get started and gleefully spies a child with a plaster under his chin.

I advise him to wait for the next one as it is a difficult age and site. Stitching small squirming children can be like trying to thread a needle on a bucking bronco.

And this is not my first rodeo.

The next laceration is perfect for teaching. It is straight and sited on an obliging adult. My student puts on sterile gloves and I tell him to give the local anaesthetic slowly to minimise the burn.

He gives it magnificently slowly and I am reminded of a praying mantis. He is very thin and has huge, wide-set eyes. He hovers over the patient in a trance-like state and takes no less than a minute to pick up the suture needle with the needle holder. It is painfully clumsy to watch, and I worry that the local will wear off before we begin.

I tell him to place the first stitch in the middle of the laceration in order to match up the edges.

Looping and tying the stitch is even more time-consuming and I wonder whether he has a coordination problem. My patience wears out after just one stitch.

'Ok, that's good for your first time,' I say and commandeer the draped tray. He looks crestfallen but it is a long laceration, and, at this rate, it will heal before we stitch it.

As I complete the last stitch, a man in a smouldering suit staggers into the ED. His hair and beard are smoking, and he wheezes and coughs, colliding with nursing staff and patients in the corridor. He dropped a cigarette on the floor of his car, which had been recently fitted with some kind of gas canister to provide a turbo boost. The car exploded right outside the hospital and he is, literally, on fire.

I guide him into the shower in the doctor's restroom, unclip the moon bag from around my waist, and step in with him. I turn the cold on full and the stench of his burning beard is quelled.

Luckily, the burns to his skin are not too bad but his tongue is like a charred black leaf in his mouth and he is wheezing so he will need admission for inhalation burns. I can see that the receptionist, who is a heavy smoker, is trying to get a moment alone with him. I wonder if there is a problem with his medical aid but then I hear her asking him where he is buying cigarettes. They are still not legally available even though we have progressed to level three.

There is never a dull moment. I change into dry scrubs and put my running shoes out on the shirking wall to dry off. I see the next patient in my socks. He is an advocate and his opening words are 'I think that I am having a nervous breakdown.'

I usually stand at the foot of the bed while I take down the history but, for this one, I pull up a chair. I hide my socked feet under me, but I soon see that he is too distraught to notice my attire.

It transpires that this articulate and very anxious man attended a few months of law school before his father was retrenched and it became clear that he would not be able to pay the fees. The young man left university and got a job as a legal clerk.

It started slowly, giving advice to people and studying judgments, but sooner or later he represented a client in court. The client did not have money to pay for formal legal counsel and, he assured himself, it was just this once. But he went from strength to strength, taking more work on board and winning landmark cases. He had married another advocate and their children were at a private school.

He knew that what he was doing was wrong, but he just got deeper and deeper in.

Until, unbeknown to him, he was nominated as a judge. As part of the routine screening, his academic transcripts were requested.

The fact that he had not attended law school nor passed the bar exam has exploded his life.

He is so ashamed. He cannot eat or drink. He feels ill.

He is also facing prison time as it is a criminal offence to masquerade as a professional before a judge. All the landmark cases that he had won would have to be retried. His children cannot face their schoolmates. His wife is stunned and even his parents are bewildered by this turn of events. They thought that he had got his degree by correspondence.

'I never actually told anyone that I was an advocate, but I never denied it either.' He sinks his head into his hands, and I feel really sorry for him. His hair is filthy, and his eyes are bloodshot. I am not sure what I can do to help him; maybe he just needs to talk.

I am reminded of French François. The difference is that people will die if you pretend to be a doctor whereas the judge makes the decision in a legal case. The advocate just presents the argument. Maybe I am justifying his actions because I feel so sorry for him.

I think that this guy is a high risk for suicide and so I try to convince him to be admitted to the hospital. He refuses to even consider it and I am faced with a dilemma. He came in alone and the only way that I can force him to stay in the hospital is to declare him a danger to himself and get the police involved. As there is a warrant out for his arrest, I may be doing him a disservice by doing this. He refuses to give me numbers for anyone in his family and expressly forbids me to discuss anything further with them. I offer to refer him to a therapist and give him a script for an antidepressant. I doubt that either of these interventions can save him now.

What a terrible tale of woe he has brought upon himself.

Thirty-Four

I hear a Cape robin chirping merrily in the half-light and I lie in bed and ponder where the world is going. Now that we have locked down, we are going to have to make decisions about how to open again. The gears are grinding smaller and smaller and it feels like we are getting entangled.

Countries that seemed to be on top of the pandemic are having a recurrence of positives. There seems to be no end in sight.

The medical profession has taken fright and is turning on itself, putting out more and more rules and hurdles to patient care as the fear of litigation grows. Urgent surgeries are being delayed because of fear and ignorance. A few of my older colleagues have taken early retirement, heeding the call for older individuals to minimise their risk. Doctors in the ED are reluctant to examine patients with any sign of infection and diagnoses are being missed.

You will never pick up appendicitis or a perforated ulcer while standing in the doorway.

There is still a sense of dullness in the world. Although the light is bright, nothing seems shiny anymore.

When I leave for work the snoopies are lined up on the lawn. They are soaking in the morning sunlight like a row of glossy chess pieces. I make a mental note to measure them up for new winter coats. They have very thin fur and they hate the cold. Jake's teeth are actually chattering. I glance at them as I leave and am struck again by how neat they are; their smooth brindle, black and white sharp against the golden grass. They remind me of Timone.

Timone was a meerkat that was abandoned by his family. Perhaps he would have been called a meerkitten when the snoopies and I found him, alone and terrified, on the edge of a field on our farm. He was a tiny, busy bundle of fur and I was amazed at how well the snoopies tolerated his antics. He could run right over their sleeping bodies and play with the white tips of their whippy tails for hours.

In the entrance hall of the farmhouse there is a wall hung with my favourite photographs. I have a beautiful picture of Timone, taken just before he died. He is watching the sunset and his shadow is massive on the red sand behind him. It was almost as if he knew his time with us was coming to an end.

He was unbearably cute, with low-slung, cupped ears and an almost-human face. He would jump onto the bed as the sun came up and sit on the duvet, facing east through the window and warm his chest in the rising sun. His little arms hung by his sides in a typical upright stance. I have such a clear image of his little wise face and his body bathed in the soft morning light.

He was a dear addition to our family. He was free to go, but he chose not to; unlike Merle, an adolescent crow with a broken wing, who lived with us for a few weeks while she healed. She would look at me with a cold, beady eye and I knew she longed for her freedom. She was just biding her time. As soon as she could fly, she was gone to join her parents who had been wheeling in the air around the farmhouse during her convalescence.

Timone was part of the pack, running along amongst the loping pack of dogs. He would stop and scratch in the cracked earth for ants and other delights, and then bound on again, his furry tail aloft as he chirped and whistled to his adopted family.

Sadly he had a seizure and died. I miss him with a sore heart.

It feels like the government is turning on its people. Citizens are being arrested for petty or non-existent transgressions and some people fear the police more than they fear the virus.

I listen to Simon and Garfunkel on my commute. The rolling guitar chords and wistful lyrics suit my mood. It is a proper winter morning and the highway is a stream of ruby tail lights ahead of me. I wonder what a turnpike is.

There is a long line of people waiting to access the hospital. Technology is an amazing thing. Instead of waiting in the queue, I send a text to the hospital group and get a link on my mobile. I fill in my details and get quizzed as regards my risk factors. I am sure that I am high risk, but if I answer 'yes' to any of the questions, I won't be allowed access to the facility. It is a bit like those questionnaires that ask the same question in different ways in order to assess what kind of personality you have.

I sit in the car with the heater on and the music playing until I get a clearance email and then I bypass the queue and scan the code. Pretty nifty, I think.

The incidence of injuries while baking has increased exponentially during lockdown. Finger lacerations, burns and exploding pressure cookers are among the reasons for visiting me. Today a young man walks in with a dish towel over his hand. When I lift the towel up, I find that his middle finger is rotated completely around, so that the fingernail is facing the palm. It looks horrendous and I swallow back an involuntary gasp.

He was using an electric food mixer and the little string at the top of the bag of flour got twisted around the whisk and his finger. His finger is definitely broken but I am not sure which way to rotate it to set it right. I take a photograph and forward it to the plastic surgeon, who agrees to take the young chef to the theatre and repair the finger. Luckily, the patient has not eaten today, so they can take him immediately. I arrange everything but five minutes later the plastic surgeon calls me back.

'The patient needs to have a Covid swab.'

'He has no symptoms of Covid,' I reassure him, 'and the swab will take more than 12 hours to come back. He will have already gone home by then.'

'Yes, I know,' the plastic surgeon says. 'but the theatre staff and the hospital need to document the patient's status. It is the new hospital policy.'

This seems a crazy waste of time and resources to me. I cannot see how it is going to change the management of cases. They cannot delay the surgery until they have the Covid result as he will lose his finger. So, we all just have to wear masks and wash our hands. If the swab result comes back positive tomorrow, what difference will it make to what we have done today? I have already seen him and examined his finger. Surely the surgeon will not be closer to him than I have been. And the one thing that we do know about this virus is that, unlike leprosy and TB, it does not take hours of exposure to get infected.

The lack of logic is frustrating. But the plastic surgeon won't take the patient to the theatre until he has been swabbed so back into the gown and mask I go, and into the room, armed with a giant ear bud to put up his nose. Once the swab is done, the patient will go to theatre. Re-implantation of a finger is very time sensitive and the anaesthetist will be doing a crash induction on this one.

Thirty-Five

ew files are waiting in the tray. Before I can pick one up,
the door swings open and an elderly man walks in. He is
holding a tea towel against the left side of his chest. His
face is grey, and I think 'heart attack'. I guide him towards the
resuscitation area and start getting a history as we walk.

'What's up?' I ask casually.

'It came out here.' Moving the little towel to the side, I see a
pomegranate jewel of blood just below his collar bone. There are a
few red spots on his open-necked shirt.

Not a heart attack then.

'And in over here.' He lifts the shirt at the back and shows me
a similar little round mark on his back. I stare for a second before
asking the obvious.

'What is "it"?'

'It was a metal stake. In the garden. I lost my balance and fell
back on it. I was stuck there for a while and my neighbour heard me
calling so he came and pulled me off.'

'Your neighbour pulled you off a metal stake in the garden? The
stake went through your chest? Did you come in an ambulance
or did your neighbor bring you?' Even as I ask, I wonder at the
relevance of the last question.

'Oh no, he's too old to drive! I took a taxi.'

'Can you just lie down on this bed for me?' I hustle him onto the
first bed in the resuscitation area and start putting up a drip.

A portable chest X-ray does not show any leak of air or blood into his lung space, which is an enormous relief. I seem more relieved than he does, but that is probably because he doesn't know much about the placement of vital organs inside his body. A CT scan with contrast shows the air-filled tract where the spike has been, located precisely between the subclavian artery and vein. They form three rings – one black with air and the other two white with contrast – directly touching each other. The stake had gone between the two like an arrow through a tight fork in a tree.

If he were a cat, he would have used up one of his nine lives.

Cats are featured today as the next file is a Workmen's Compensation patient who has been bitten by a cat. Delivery workers, security guards and police are often bitten by dogs in their line of work but incurring a cat bite is unusual unless the patient works for an animal shelter.

This man is an electrician who ordered a distribution board from a factory across town. A feral cat had climbed into the box while it was standing open and it was then sealed and transported. By the time the electrician unpacked the board, the cat was really freaked out. It flew out of the box and bit the electrician on his forearm as it shot past him. It is quite a bad bite and needs an anti-tetanus shot and antibiotics. Because the cat is feral, he will need a course of four vaccinations for rabies. He tells me that this is very inconvenient. I tell him that getting rabies will be more inconvenient.

A colleague working at a clinic outside Johannesburg saw a patient who was bitten by his own cat. The cat was sitting on the doorstep, he picked it up and it attacked him. Apparently, it savaged him so ferociously that he struck the cat against the wall to make it let go of his arm. The cat was dead, and the patient was beside himself. The cat was definitely vaccinated against rabies, but the bites were so severe and atypical, and the death of the cat seemed inappropriate so the doctor asked for a copy of the vaccination certificate. When the patient came in the following day for a dressing change and check of the wound, the certificate was inspected. The cat had been vaccinated religiously, every year.

The doctor gave a course of antibiotics and brought the patient back for regular wound reviews. Healing was slow and the follow-ups dragged on for weeks. The arm was still red, and the patient had a low-grade temperature. The doctor tried a different course of antibiotics.

A few weeks later the patient went home early from work as he wasn't feeling well. There, waiting on the doorstep, was his cat.

In that horrible moment he realised that the cat that attacked him had not been his cat. It had been a cat that looked just like his. And therefore, there was no vaccination record for that cat. He went back to the hospital, but it was too late. He had already contracted rabies and he died a few days later.

There was a huge outcry. Why had the patient not been vaccinated? The simple answer is that my colleague believed that there was no need to vaccinate the patient as the animal was covered for rabies. Who would have thought that he was attacked by an identical cat?

There is no treatment for rabies – it is the most fatal virus known to mankind. Once contracted, the chance of survival is almost zero. As a child I had read it up in my *Family Doctor* book. It used to be called hydrophobia because the virus multiplies in the salivary glands and also causes spasm of the muscles used to swallow. The patient is terribly thirsty but choking on their own saliva. *The Family Doctor* had hand-drawn pictures of frenzied people being restrained. It made a lasting impression on me and I spent my childhood on the look-out for rabid animals.

Ironically, as a teenager, I did actually come into contact with rabies. On the farm a jackal was hanging about in the shade of a big tree. It was too close to the house to be normal behaviour for a jackal in broad daylight, and it was panting and staggering in circles. My father called the state vet, who suspected rabies. He shot the jackal and set about taking out the brain for testing.

Being intrigued by such matters, I held the skull as the vet cut it in half with a hacksaw. I remember the jackal's grey fur and pointy nose as he lay dead on the lawn. He seemed so small and harmless. I was holding the skull open so that the vet could get the brain out and my fingertip was nipped by a sharp edge of bone. It broke the glove and nicked my skin.

A few weeks later the vet called the farm to confirm that the jackal was positive for rabies. He suggested that I go to the doctor.

I went to the local general practitioner and told him the story. He reassured me, telling me that there was no risk unless I had been bitten. Years later, at medical school, I found out that exposure to cerebro-spinal fluid was an equal, if not higher risk, than the saliva of a rabid animal. Worse, rabies could have a prolonged incubation period of up to seven years. I recall sitting in that lecture hall and calculating how many years had passed. I felt distinctly restless and hydrophobic.

Rabies means madness in Latin and can present with anxiety and agitated behaviour or stupor. The virus is called a Lyssavirus, with Lyssa meaning violent in Greek. These facts were not in *The Family Doctor*, which was probably published in about 1930.

Rabies can infect any warm-blooded mammal from a bite, scratch or lick from an infected animal. It travels in the nerves to the brain and then to the salivary glands, where it multiplies and readies itself for further transmission. It is extremely infectious and, without vaccination and immunoglobulin, almost always fatal. To date fewer than 20 people worldwide have ever survived a confirmed diagnosis of rabies.

I give the electrician his first rabies shot and send him on his way with a course of antibiotics and dressings.

There are six files waiting in the tray. I waste time counting them and looking at the main complaint on the front of each one. Dizziness comes second only to numbness as my least favourite complaint. They are both such non-specific symptoms and require an enormous range of tests to exclude any serious cause. It is much easier to X-ray a limb or write a prescription for an obvious infection. There is also a general body weakness awaiting me, and a fever.

There are no sisters to bring in the next patient, so I open the door to the waiting room and call him myself. He is sitting miserably in the corner, something small protruding from his mouth. It looks like a short stick. Perhaps the triage sister forgot to remove the thermometer. He comes into an exam room and ruefully shows me a cable tie that he has fastened around one of his molars in an attempt to pull it out. The end of the cable tie is sticking out of the corner of his mouth. I get a scalpel and try to cut it off.

I am reminded of a young man who came in with a zipper stuck on his eyelid. He tried to loosen it but succeeded only in catching more fragile skin in the meshed teeth. He told me that the zipper was on the collar of his sweater and I hoped that was true. The alternative was too awful to contemplate.

He cut the zip and a little piece of material off the sweater and came to the ED. Once I had finished, I woke him from the sedation and said, 'It's off.' He looked into my eyes and sleepily declared, 'I love you.' It was so easy.

The cable tie is not so easy. I can't believe that the thin strip of plastic is so difficult to cut. After sawing backwards and forwards against the side of the tooth for 10 minutes I must give up and refer it to the maxillo-facial surgeon. It feels like an absurd referral.

Thirty-Six

On Monday morning I am at my post before six. When I left the farm, the moon was still high in the sky and the horizon was black and freckled with stars.

The parking lot is grey in the half-light of dawn. The shirking wall and my patch of lawn are crusted in frost. There are no smokers as the government has ruled that cigarettes are still banned under level three. I wonder what that is really all about.

The ED has been unnaturally quiet during lockdown but this morning I walk into chaos. Before dawn, the local bowling club was set alight. Arson is suspected as the windows were smashed, and the patio furniture torched. The flames quickly spread into the building, where nine people who work for the club were sleeping.

Eight escaped with only minor burns but one had to jump from the window of the second floor and he has more than 90 per cent burns. The night doctor is struggling to stabilise him, and he looks enormously relieved to see me. I put my bag down and get busy with a kit called an intraosseous. This is a little drill that places a cannula directly into the patient's bone marrow. All of the burn victim's skin has peeled off and there is no other way to get fluids or medications into him.

We will need to sedate him in order to intubate him before his airway swells shut. He will need pain medication and lots of fluids. Once we get him stable, a helicopter will take him to the closest trauma hospital with a burns unit. Even with specialised care, he has almost no chance of survival.

Before I can make tea or soup, I have to see the other eight people who are lined up in the cubicles. It is 6.30 am, but I tell the night doctor that he might as well go. There is no point in him starting with patients that he will just end up handing over to me. I will see them from the beginning and then at least I will know who they are.

What a gruesome start to my day; and it goes from bad to worse. There is hooting and shouting outside and a man runs through the double doors with an unconscious child in his arms. He throws the child on the ground in the corridor of the ED with a panicked cry.

There is a moment of startled silence as all the heads in the ED turn towards the commotion, and it takes a few seconds before I realise that the child is not breathing. The sisters and I lift the boy quickly onto the closest bed and start CPR. While doing chest compressions, I ask one of the team to get some history from the man who brought him in. She comes back and tells me that the child drowned in the bath.

This seems highly improbable to me. He is quite a big boy – we guess he is about 12 – and his skin and hair are not wet. He is not cold to the touch, but his face is a bit mottled. There are no external signs of injury. His pupils are fixed and dilated, and I suspect that he has been dead for more than 20 minutes. I ask the sister to go back out and get more information from the man.

A patient's history is extremely important, especially in an attempted resuscitation. We need to figure out why his heart has stopped if we are to have any hope of restarting it. While many adults go into cardiac arrest from an underlying heart problem, children usually go into cardiac arrest because of a primary respiratory cause. In a case of drowning, especially if the child is still cold from the water, we could continue CPR for hours. It seems that submersion in cold water triggers a mammalian diving instinct, which pools all the oxygen in the body and keeps the brain viable for much longer than we initially thought possible. But this does not look like a drowning to me. I ask if there was any medication in the house that the boy could have taken. The answer comes back a definite no.

The sister now tells me that the child was not actually in the bath; he was found lying next to it, but the man – now established to be his uncle – still thinks that he drowned. The boy is 10 years old and he was alone in the bathroom with his brother, who is also 10. I ask if they are twins, but no, they are cousins.

The next question is whether the boy was breathing when he was found and if anyone did CPR? No to both of those. And how far away do they live? The uncle gives the name of a suburb which is at least 10 minutes' drive away, not counting the time taken to get the boy into the car. Things are not looking good.

Throughout all the confusion we are doing CPR and checking for any returning sign of life. I know it is hopeless, but we have to try. I let a sister take over chest compressions and I go to fetch the sonar machine. Putting the probe on his skinny chest I can see his heart easily and there is no sign of activity. I go back to the head of the bed and check his pupils again. Fixed and dilated. No corneal reflex, no movement of the eyes when I turn his head. They stay staring fixed forward, dead as a cheap doll. I ask the sister to get me some iced water from the dispensing machine outside. She looks at me doubtfully, wondering if I need refreshments, but I want to squirt it into the boy's ears to check for any sign of residual brain activity.

Nothing.

My heart is heavy when I tell the team to stop CPR. We have tried for half an hour and there is no point. With brain death and no cardiac activity, it is still possible to harvest some of the non-vital organs for transplant purposes. A question flashes into my head about the origin of the term 'vital'. I have always assumed that it means we cannot live without them, but perhaps it means that they cannot live without blood supply. Kidneys, liver and heart are out; but cornea and skin and bone can be transplanted quite long after the heart stops beating.

I don't know if a 10-year-old would be eligible for transplant donation and how one could begin that conversation with a family. I have never had an unsuccessful resuscitation on a 10-year-old before. Anyway, a transplant is out of the question as I remind myself that this is an unnatural death and so the boy will have to go for a post-mortem. My thoughts are swirling around and getting tangled. I must accept that there is nothing to be salvaged from this dismal situation. I take off my gloves and ask the sisters if the rest of the family has arrived.

The worst part is yet to come.

There is no easy way to tell a mother that her child is dead. I sit miserably on the bed next to her as she screams and cries. I pat her shoulder and try not to fold my arms in front of me. My body is leaden with sorrow for the ripples of misery that will radiate out into the world from this one event. Like a giant railroad switch, the steel points clang and the train of this family's existence swerves onto an entirely new course.

At the back of my mind, I wonder what the two boys were up to in the bathroom in the middle of the morning. I suspect that the other boy knows exactly what happened, but somehow, I doubt that he will tell. Guilty or ashamed, he may hold out in the hope of forensic science missing the dreadful truth. Whatever it is, I am sure that he has no idea how heavy a dark secret can be.

I have reached the point in my life where, if someone asks, 'Should I tell you a secret?' I simply answer 'No, thanks.' Keeping secrets alienates me from myself, and not keeping them is worse. There are secrets that I have carried for almost half a century and there seems no point in telling them now. Nevertheless, my life would have been easier without the weight of them.

Thinking about it, I wonder if knowing secrets was an unconscious driver in my aspiring to be a spy when I was a child. I wanted unequivocal access to the truth, and it was a sad day for me when I realised that the truth is almost always subjective. Also, the more information I held, the higher my risk of being silenced would be. Spies and agents are always on the run and are inherently duplicitous. On the surface of it, joining the circus and becoming a trapeze artist would be a simpler career path.

Thirty-Seven

There is still no antibody test to see if we have immunity to the Coro Coro. A fellow doctor, who was positive for coronavirus and is now negative, is on a clinical trial. They are taking blood from people who have recovered and trying to isolate antibodies to donate to patients who are really sick. She posts a link on the hospital group and I read it with interest.

Donors must have fully recovered from the virus and, if female, they cannot ever have been pregnant. This is because of an unusual complication called TRALI, which can happen after receiving any blood product transfusion. The acronym stands for transfusion-related acute lung injury and it is a life-threatening reaction in a recipient of a blood product. It seems that antibodies in the donated blood attack the lung of the person receiving the blood or platelets. TRALI is more common if the blood donor was a woman who has previously been pregnant. It is a chance we take with all transfusions, but it is of particular relevance in Covid as the receiving patient is already in acute respiratory distress and any exacerbating factors must be avoided

I am not eligible to join the trial as all my coronavirus tests have been negative. I remain convinced that I have had it and would be very interested to test for antibodies.

But I will have to wait.

The next patient got into an altercation with a helicopter blade. I am relieved to hear that it was a model helicopter, not a full-sized one, but it has still done some real damage to his hands and arms. He is a very healthy 80-year-old who has built and flown model aeroplanes and helicopters most of his life. He decided to make use of the lockdown to get a few models out of storage and start working on them. Somehow, the rotor switched on while he and the helicopter were confined in his workshop. It started hovering towards him and he raised his arms to defend himself.

The wounds on his forearms and hands are textbook defence wounds – a pattern of lacerations on the little finger side of the arm typical of victims trying to protect their face and neck from assailants with sharp objects. These lacerations are much deeper than would usually be made by a human with a knife or a bottle; several of them right down to the bone and have severed tendons and muscles in their path. He is spattered with blood and has tied compression bandages over the worst wounds. I can just imagine the helicopter rising up and looming over him, hacking away like some kind of horror movie.

The disrupted tendons, as we call it, will have to be repaired in the operating theatre, but the wounds are bleeding too much for me to leave them without stitching. The worst is over the knuckle of the index finger of his right hand, where the joint space is chopped open. The finger has almost been amputated and the blood is flowing like a river.

I am quick with sutures, but this is going to take a while. I count nine lacerations and they are all jagged and deep. I pull up a chair and adjust the bed.

'Comfortable?' I ask him, making brief eye contact over the top of my glasses.

'Yep,' he answers. He is very calm and a pleasure to work with, but I need to hurry along as all of the wounds are bleeding briskly. I ask the sister to hold the pressure on the left arm and I start on the right.

When he is all stitched up, he will go for X-rays and then be admitted for the tendon repairs. I explain all of this to him while

I work and then ask about the model planes and helicopters. He is very knowledgeable and obviously passionate about the subject and I find myself asking questions and learning all kinds of new information. The conversation carries us both for almost an hour and I give him his anti-tetanus jab and dispatch him down to X-rays.

The next patient is waiting on the other side of the screen. Brought in by ambulance, I listened with half an ear to the handover while I was stitching. It seems that the patient was crossing the street and an advertising trailer blew over and crushed him. Over the past few years, trailers fitted with A-frame advertising boards can be found at many major intersections. The advertising board acts like a sail; a strong gust of wind lifted the trailer off its wheels then dropped it on this young man.

I wash the glove powder from my hands and take off my glasses. Picking up the file, I move the mobile table with me into the cubicle and start to make notes.

'Hi. I am Doctor Anne. Sorry to keep you waiting a bit.' My standard greeting, even if the patient has only waited a minute. 'Where are you injured?'

'Just here on the corner of Main street and Ninth,' he answers.

'No, I mean, where on your body are you injured?' I try not to laugh. He looks very stressed.

'My back. I can't move my legs.'

I lift the blanket and touch the front of his legs lightly.

'Can you feel this?'

'No. And I can't move them either.' He looks sick with worry. I work my way up from his feet, checking for movement, sensation and reflexes. My examination concludes that he has damaged his spine at about the sixth thoracic vertebra. This is exactly where the sharp edge of the trailer hit him. A CT scan will confirm fractures and any damage to the cord. I tell him not to eat or drink until we have done the imaging in case there is something that can be repaired. I fill in the forms for the scan and slap on his sticker at the top. I see that it is a Workmen's Compensation file and my heart sinks. I turn back to the bed.

'Why were you on the road? Do you work there? Like a newspaper salesman or cutting the grass?' I ask hopefully.

'No, it is lunchtime and I was going to the shops.'

Oh dear. My eyes go to the paramedic, who is flirting with the nurse. 'If he was running across the road during his lunchtime, I'm afraid it is not going to qualify as a Workmen's Comp.'

The paramedic shrugs. 'The employer said it will be covered. He's on his way in to fill in the forms.'

I am an old dog in the ED, and I know most of the tricks. 'Sorry, but you are going to have to wait until we see if the hospital accepts it as Workmen's Comp,' I tell the paramedic. 'Because I suspect that it is not going to, in which case he is a private patient and the hospital will give a quote, which the patient or the company will have to accept and pay before he can be admitted.'

'What?' I can see that the paramedic is totally irritated, but not nearly as irritated as I will be if I find out that the employer is going to weasel out paying for him.

I explain to the patient. 'Workmen's Compensation only covers injuries that happen at work. If you are driving to or from work or leave the premises for some reason other than work, then you are not covered. Unless your job is to be on the road, like a driver or a street cleaner or whatever. The problem is that you seem to have a serious injury which will need investigations and treatment. It is not just an ED consult; I am pretty sure that you have damaged your spinal cord, and this will need scans and operations and extensive rehabilitation. It will be very expensive.'

And, here is the kicker. Once the paramedics leave the patient in the ED of a private facility, the ED doctor in question must get a specialist doctor in government to accept the patient. Taking the patient from one hospital to another needs consent from the accepting doctor before the interhospital ambulance will take the patient. This is because there are often no beds or unwilling staff on the receiving end and they simply block the paramedics from offloading the patient.

This young man will fall under the care of a neurosurgeon and I have never, in almost 30 years of practice, managed to find a bed to transfer a neurosurgery patient from private to government. Be it laziness, belligerence or exhaustion, they just say no.

But if the paramedic takes the patient straight to a government casualty, then they are obliged to see the patient and cannot turn them away. It is a ridiculous system, but I have become wise to it and I am not accepting this patient until the issue of payment has been clarified.

It turns out that there is no way we are going to get this through under Workmen's Compensation and the paramedic reloads the patient, still restrained on a spine board, and, muttering loudly, sets off for the government hospital down the road.

Thirty-Eight

Today the numbers are showing the trends in the pandemic that we have expected. We have admitted 10 or more Covid pneumonias today and the waiting room is humming with more. For some reason, our profile of acutely ill patients is still not following the international norms. We are seeing young and old, with and without pre-existing conditions all bundled together.

Honestly, I am awed by my profession. Nurses and doctors, physiotherapists and physicians' assistants are stepping up to the line and facing the virus. Two months ago our eyes were wide with fear – and they probably still are – but everyone is pulling their weight. The pulmonologists are at the centre of the storm and the patients are piling up for them. They work diligently at our sides in the ED, covering themselves with layers of protection and then going into the rooms with the sick patients, examining them and managing them to the best of their ability.

A few weeks ago, all acutely ill respiratory patients were admitted as a Person Under Investigation – a PUI – but now we are seeing people who tell us on the telephone that they know that they are positive and need to come in. We are using our outside room and shipping containers converted into isolation wards, but everyone is being seen in time and, touching wood, we have had no deaths. Yet.

It makes me proud to be a member of this team. One of the older physicians has a heart to heart with me this evening and tells me that he has done his will and got his affairs in order. As a group, the pulmonologists know that they will be at ground zero in this pandemic. Some will get sick and some will die, yet they are here, answering our calls for help. Knowing the danger and still showing up – that is proper courage.

I still can't figure out why certain areas are much harder hit with what is supposed to be the same virus. The numbers of admissions and deaths in the Western Cape remain higher than anywhere else in the country. Maybe they are testing more people or have a more reliable system of reporting; maybe it is a different strain of Coronavirus. Maybe it is the altitude?

It is 7 am and I am at my post. I have a Tupperware of leftover lentil stew to sustain me for the day. With no sign of the coffee shop reopening, I must prepare meals at home for my shifts. One good thing about the pandemic is that it stops the impulsive buying of sweets to bolster flagging energy. I am also tallying up Continuing Medical Education points, attending various online meetings and webinars. Mostly, these are about Covid 19 but there are a few other interesting topics mixed in.

Today, I see an article addressing the demographics of coronavirus. It must be almost impossible to divide out socio-economic factors versus genetic predisposition. False reporting early in the South African pandemic stated that it was a white person's disease, probably based on the groups of travellers coming in from Europe and the US, many of whom were white. These kinds of reports are dangerous on several levels, but today I see an interesting theory explaining why many of the victims of serious illness in Scandinavian countries were dark-skinned.

It seems that underlying vitamin D deficiency may predispose a person to a serious coronavirus infection. Elderly people, especially those residing in care homes, often do not get enough sunlight for their skin to make vitamin D. Interestingly, melanin also protects the skin from sunlight and so, people with dark skin who are living in an area with less sunlight than they would get in an equatorial country can become vitamin D deficient.

The medical profession is scrambling to understand this disease and come up with some solutions.

A bell sounds over the public announcement system in the hospital. It is the kind of bing-bong that precedes an announcement in the arrivals hall at the airport, but there is no voice message to follow. After the bells have been rung three times, I realise that this occurs hourly. On the fourth bell, a nurse comes around with hand sanitiser and sprays us all. Another follows with a disinfectant solution for all the surfaces. I am watching them scurry about when the triage nurse comes to tell me that there is a very pale man waiting in the triage queue outside the ED. She is worried that he might be sick. I go out of the double doors and spy the patient in question. He is very old and very pale. He looks like a wax statue, slumped in a wheelchair. I think that he looks dead, from here, but they must certainly bring him to the front of the queue.

I quickly don a new set of gown, gloves, apron, mask and visor while the sisters hustle the wax statue onto the bed in resus. Yep, he's dead as a doornail. I wonder what a doornail is and why it is deader than any other kind of nail. While I am still checking for signs of life, a strange man appears in the room. He is wearing a complete space suit with a pipe protruding from the top. It looks like a handle.

'Is he dead, doctor?' He asks.

'Yes,' I reply, bemused by his appearance.

He whips out a roll of plastic and, with the assistance of the sister, deftly shrouds the body. Then he wraps him in duct tape from head to foot and does another two layers. Before I can even inform the family, the body is magically whisked away.

It seems that Handle Head is summoned to all deaths of suspected or confirmed Covid-19 in the hospital and is tasked with limiting contamination and taking the body away to a dedicated mortuary.

The bell chimes. People appear to spray us.

I feel like Alice in Wonderland.

During a break, I call the forensic pathologist to find out what she found on the post-mortem on the 10-year-old boy. She tells me that she can find no macroscopic cause of death. No drowning, no electric shock, nothing to be seen with the naked eye. She has sent blood and tissue away for toxicology but it will be a long time before those results come back. So far there are no answers.

Thirty-Nine

Today we had the first Covid deaths at our hospital. Not just one, but four in a row. Three were young people that I had admitted over the past few days. They had no other medical problems and presented with flu-like symptoms and shortness of breath. Their oxygen saturation was low, and their chest X-rays slapped me with reality. They showed fluffy white patches, like cotton wool, blotting out the normal blackness of air-filled lung tissue

Covid is here, it shouted.

The three patients were admitted, along with a few others, and they were all doing relatively well. Then suddenly, on Monday morning, all three died within 10 minutes of each other.

Just like that.

Devastating.

The fourth patient was well into her 90s and was admitted for another medical problem. She had a routine coronavirus swab, which came back positive, but I think it was incidental. She died with coronavirus, not because of it.

It is not just statistics now, but real people who have been under my care. Frightening, but also to be expected. We knew that this was coming; we just held out a tiny hope that it wouldn't.

Protective equipment is running low and the hospital is full. There are no beds but somehow, we are managing not to turn anyone away. There is pandemonium as more than half the staff are positive and have been booked off. The remaining staff is under such pressure that I am sure we will get sick soon.

Behind closed doors there is a discussion about closing the hospital. There is a minimum number of staff that we need in order to stay afloat . I am privy to this discussion as I sit on the Physicians Advisory Board. The hospital is reluctant to allow the patient-staff ratio to get out of hand. There are loads of medico-legal difficulties down that road, but is it better to close your doors than to run the risk of being sued? The management thinks it might be but the doctors disagree.

Hospitals are businesses and the doctors who work there are not the decision makers.

In the early afternoon I hear that the head of the physicians' board, and the most senior pulmonologist, has flu-like symptoms. I send a laboratory technician to swab him and we push his test to the front of the queue. By mid-evening we all know that he is positive. He is not sick enough to warrant admission, but the hospital feels a bit rudderless without him. He has been the go-to person for protocols and advice since the start of the pandemic.

It seemed inevitable that he would get sick and we discussed it only yesterday. He has been looking after more than 30 Covid-positive patients in high care and ICU over the past few weeks. One of the younger physicians has taken over the reins but there is not much that she can do without staff.

The gloves are running short and I am wearing a shoe cover on my head as the hats are finished.

How will we know when we have peaked? Whether considering physical prowess or waves of viral infection, I think that one can only recognise the peak once it has passed. As of the end of June, there were around 150,000 recorded positive cases and almost 3,000,000 deaths. Virologists are saying that the testing probably picks up about 10 per cent of the actual numbers. That would mean that about one-and-a-half million people have probably had it. It leaves a lot of people still to get it.

I suppose that when the numbers start to decline, we will have passed the peak. But I suspect that there will be more peaks, like waves in an ocean, surging and troughing for a long time to come.

The government is reconsidering lockdown.

I think that this is the coldest winter that we have had in many years. An icy wind howls day and night, straight off the snow on the mountains and across the bleak plain that is the Highveld. The light is bent by blue-grey snow clouds scudding across the sky and the tan lawns are blanketed in crisp frost every morning.

Summer feels an exceptionally long way away. It is hard to relinquish my warm bed every morning before dawn, especially to come to the feverish, coughing ED full of people with the virus.

Almost every single test that we do now is positive. The printer hums and spews paper after paper, all with asterisks and hash tags highlighting the results. We are supposed to call patients back with their swab results, but that amounts to more than 50 calls a day and there is only one doctor on duty. I would outsource it to one of the sisters but with our staff numbers down to half, all hands are needed to manage the people in the unit.

I am still standing but I am not sure why. Either I am very lucky, or I have a brutal immune system. Maybe a bit of both.

I can hear the wind howling outside the double doors of the ED. I hunt down a paper cup in which to make tea. At least the unit has given up on the idea of putting patients in the containers outside, which are without electricity and heating. Since everyone is testing positive anyway, we might as well just let them all in.

Forty

For the first time in my medical career, I am tired of seeing sick people. I have had enough of patients coughing and oozing germs from every surface. I have seen too many heart-stopping chest X-rays and 'happy hypoxics' – a term coined by the physicians for patients who look fairly well even though they have a blood oxygen level not compatible with consciousness. And the worst thing is that there is no end in sight. I am the front line in the ED for the next six days from 6 am until 3 pm.

For sure, things are going to get worse.

I used to love the early shift, it gave me time to walk the snoopies in the afternoon and attend to a few things before nightfall. But now, any shift seems too much. My workplace is a battlefield and my dreams are full of wars, troops and terrified generals. The terrains are shifting, bizarre is becoming the new normal and night terrors are strewn with gruesome deaths.

It is mid-July and the wind howls around the farmhouse. Branches scratch the tin roof and the timbers groan as they are buffeted.

It is a morning for Pink Floyd. I'm in the mood for some cynicism and paranoia. Their music is a different kind of poetry to Leonard Cohen and is reminiscent of my high school years. I know the lyrics by heart and, more than 30 years after *The Final Cut* was released, it feels relevant today. I listen to the whole album, ending with 'Two Suns in the Sunset' as I park and watch the bleak sunrise. I read somewhere that Nick Mason, the drummer for Pink Floyd, could not manage the complex time changes of this song and was replaced by someone else. I am early for my shift so I give the song another listen.

I don't know much about drumming, but I like their different sound here. At the moment, it feels like I don't know much about anything. A lovely saxophone solo ends the song, and, with a heavy heart, I put on my mask and make my way to my post.

I wish that I could just run away from all of this.

The night doctor hands over a 92-year-old man who was brought in by ambulance at midnight after he fell at his old age home. He has hit his head and has a painful hip. He is Covid positive, like everyone else it seems, but he has no respiratory symptoms.

Despite having been in the unit for a few hours, he has not had bloods or X-rays done yet. I go in and examine him, as I suspect that the night doctor just looked at him from the door, but I can't find much wrong with him. He has a large bump on the back of the head and pain in his right hip, so I fill in a form for a CT scan of his brain and some X-rays. I also send the basic bloods to the lab. He is the only patient in the unit when I take over, occupying pride of place in the middle resuscitation bed.

He goes down to X-rays and the three resuscitation beds fill up with another three old men, all from the Italian Old Age Home. They all have Covid and are coughing like mad. The closest one is quite short of breath but still jokes with me. I fill in forms for all of them to get the same blood tests and chest X-rays and then move along.

Knee-deep in patients now, I hear the phone at the doctors' desk ringing incessantly. When it finally stops, the one at the nurses' station starts. We are all dressed in PPE and busy with patients, so the phone goes unanswered. After a few minutes they are silent but then my mobile starts to buzz in my pocket. I glance at the screen and see that it is the senior radiologist calling.

It must be something serious.

'Hello,' I mumble through my mask. She wastes no time with niceties.

'The patient in resus has a massive pneumothorax.'

'Pneumothorax?' I repeat, as if I have never heard of such a thing. My mind flies over the three old men in resus. None of them has a history of trauma; so why would they have a collapsed lung?

Then I remember the guy who was in the resus bay when I took over. He had a history of a fall, but I sent him down to the X-ray department. He was not X-rayed in the ED. Perhaps someone could collapse their lung from excessive coughing.

'What is the patient's name?' I ask.

'There is no name on the X-ray,' she replies. 'The loaded film just says resus bay one.'

Bed one is the jovial Italian man. I trot to his bedside and check him out again. He is quite short of breath, but his air entry sounds the same on both sides. I thought that his X-ray would confirm a Covid pneumonia. I click on the computer to view the images and, indeed, his left lung is in the process of collapsing. I speed dial the cardiothoracic surgeon and ask if he can see the patient. He is driving in to work so it will be about half an hour. The patient seems stable, so I set about opening all the sets of instruments and drapes that he will need. About 10 minutes in, Mr Jovial tells me that he is not feeling so well. I glance up from the tray and see that he is very pale. His shortness of breath is worse.

Damn. This is the thing about a pneumothorax. The patient can look completely fine with a bit of chest pain and a cough and the leaking lung may not progress. You must have an eagle eye to pick up the sliver of air where the leak is. But sometimes things go pear shaped. If the tension of air building up around the collapsed lung starts to put pressure on the heart and great vessels, the patient will deteriorate and die in less than a minute.

'We have to put the drain in now.' I say to the sister. Thankfully, everything is laid out and ready. While I am giving the local anaesthetic to Mr Jovial, the sister in charge of the unit comes to tell me that the handover patient is back in the unit and he has deteriorated. He is unconscious and very short of breath.

As I make the cut between Mr Jovial's ribs, I have a moment of self-doubt. Perhaps it was Mr Handover who got a portable X-ray in the resus bay before I sent him down. Maybe he is the one with the pneumothorax. It would fit better with the history of trauma.

I reassure myself that I saw the request form for the X-ray in question; the time and the bay match Mr Jovial. Anyway, I cannot abandon my post to see Mr Handover, so I tell the unit manager to push his bed through to the resus room so that I can see him. She tells me that there are already three beds in resus so there are no bays left, but I tell her that if she is worried about him, she had better bring him into my direct line of sight.

Mr Handover is pushed through, groaning and clutching the cot sides of his bed, just as my favorite physician appears in the ED.

'Please can you help me?' I ask him, as I suture the chest drain in place. 'Please can you look at this guy? He was a handover from last night; he seemed okay when I took him over, but now he has deteriorated and I'm not sure why.'

Mr Handover has managed to turn around completely in the bed, so that his feet are where his head should be. He is gazing vacantly around, taking deep, sighing breaths and the monitors are all singing about his low oxygenation and poor saturation.

'I see that he has turned the corner,' the physician jokes with me.

'Ha ha yes. I'm not sure why, though,' I answer, 'unless he has a brain bleed. His other bloods and X-rays look pretty normal. I was a bit worried that I got his films mixed up with this guy's – he has an unexplained pneumothorax.'

The physician puts his stethoscope on Mr Handover's chest and nods sagely. 'Yup. Tension pneumothorax.'

'What?' I almost shout as I tie the last stitch on Mr Jovial.

He gives me a devilish grin as he pushes Mr Handover's bed out of the ED to take him to ICU.

'Just joking,' he calls over his shoulder as he waits for the lift.

Forty-One

On Sunday morning the setting moon is perfectly round and lemon yellow as I leave the farm. The snoopies are snug by the fire and the air outside is so cold that it feels wet. The eastern sky changes from midnight blue to burning orange and the smooth rhythm of Enya keeps me company. The city centre is a black cut-out travelling alongside me. By the time I reach the hospital the blood red sun is like a yolk on the rim of the horizon.

The icy wind is still howling, and I am not in the mood today for facing the Rona. Nevertheless, I am at my post at 6 am with my little bag of food and a bottle of water. The night doctor is tired and scratchy and has six patients to hand over. I take them graciously and make a little pile of the notes, which I will move from my right to my left as I sort them out.

He has already admitted the two sickest patients in the unit – an elderly husband and wife – to the Covid ICU and they are waiting for beds. I find their family – children and grandchildren – sitting in the doctors' room. This instantly puts me into a bad mood.

I snap at them to please put their masks over their noses properly, rather than wearing them like a chin sling. The daughter whines and says, 'I can't breathe with this mask on.'

'Well, then, you will really hate the ventilator' is my parting shot as I leave the room. I hunt down the shift leader and tell her to get them out of there. When I come back there is no sign of them, which is a relief. Family is not allowed in the ED during the pandemic and also I am quite sure they are all carrying the virus, lounging about on the chair and desk that I have to use for the rest of the day.

I think that I need some time off from the pandemic. I am constantly exhausted and unusually impatient. I am so sick of coughing people and there is no end in sight. Covid also presents with strange things, like blood clots and appendicitis and many of the elderly demented patients just stop eating and check out.

My first patient is Covid positive and developed severe abdominal pain overnight. The blood work and CT scan confirm that he has appendicitis. Whether this is related to the Covid or incidental, we now have the tricky job of taking out his appendix without infecting the staff or other patients.

There is a new surgeon covering the ED and I call him on his mobile. I hear that he is out of breath when we speak and he appears, a few minutes later, in skin-tight cycling equipment. He is easy on the eye with deep blue eyes, curly dark hair and a sensual mouth. There is an awkward moment while he waits for me to finish a call. He introduces himself and I start searching for the appendix patient's file on the chaotic surface that is my desk. Making small talk, I ask, 'So, is cycling the new big thing?'

Without batting an eye, he puts his hand on his crotch and says, 'No, this is the new big thing.'

I am speechless for a second.

'It doesn't look that big to me,' I say smoothly, finding the file and taking him to the patient to introduce them.

What kind of a thing is that to say to a colleague on first meeting them? Even more peculiar, I thought it funny rather than offensive. Maybe the virus is getting to us all.

I listen to an interesting podcast on the reasons not to rush into ventilating patients with Covid pneumonia. It is interesting but also exhausting. My shifts are taking forever to go by, and I am beginning to really hate my job.

The pandemic is following me into my dreams. At night I toss and turn, faced with impossible conundrums. I am too hot and throw off the bed covers, then awake in an icy sweat.

My nightmares are full of situations that are impossible to fix. A snoopy torn apart like a beanbag that I try to stitch together, even though I know that saving him is impossible. A father who brings his child's decapitated head upturned in a chlorine bucket, and I try to manipulate the severed neck to see the airway even though the body is lifeless next to me. When I wake, I try to understand the dreams. I am overwhelmed at work but there is a gruesome element to the nightmares that are out of keeping with the coronavirus pandemic. It is like too much responsibility has flipped a switch in my head and all the dreadful images that have accumulated over the years are rattled loose. They are flooding up from my unconscious and getting snared in the mesh of my dreamworld.

Things are unravelling. I cannot differentiate between patients behind their masks. Files are slow coming through and stickers are getting mixed up. This is compounded by the fact that everyone has a cough and shortness of breath. Everyone has Covid on the chest X-ray and their swab. It is like working in a madhouse with 50 clones of the same thing all trying to get individual attention. The sicker ones just withdraw into the work of breathing; patients are confused and angry and the staff is exhausted.

Families are not allowed to identify their dead and it is just a matter of time before we make a mistake and tell them that their next of kin has passed away when, in fact, he is still alive. They will have a memorial for Uncle George, probably online. No one in the family sees the body, and six months later they will see Uncle George at the mall.

In all this confusion, it has got to happen.

I am obsessively wiping surfaces when I hear, via the red phone, that the ambulance is bringing a priority one patient. He is unconscious. They pull into the ambulance bay and I hear the patient yelling from inside the bus.

'HaAAAHHH. HaAHHHH. Ha AAHHHH!'

They push the stretcher through the waiting room and the other patients stare in alarm. One lady scoops up her toddler and leaves. I follow the stretcher into the resus room.

'What's the story?' I ask the paramedic.

'A 50-year-old male, usually well, was on a walk with his wife and suddenly collapsed. He has been like this since we got there.'

'HaAAAHHH' The patient shouts with each exhaled breath and flails around on the bed, arms and legs uncoordinated and eyes roaming the ceiling to the left and right, unseeing.

A sudden onset like this must indicate something neurological, I think. Maybe he had a seizure and is now in the confused, postictal phase that follows. Maybe he has had a bleed into his brain. The sister tries to take blood and put up a drip, but this makes him flail harder and shout more.

'What's wrong with him, doctor?' she asks nervously.

'I don't know,' I reply. Then I add, 'Yet.' Just so that everyone thinks that I have things under control. I stare at The Shouter while I hold his arm still for the drip. Aside from shouting and being completely combative, I cannot see much wrong with him. His temperature and blood pressure are normal. His sugar is normal. He is moving all his limbs strongly to fend us off. His heart and chest sound clear. He is certainly moving air.

Once the drip is up, I give him some midazolam sedative to settle him down so that I can take a CT scan image of his brain. I am sure that I will see a bleed.

While The Shouter is in the scanner, I ask the family for any history. They tell me that he was a completely well man until he suddenly collapsed today. He has definitely not had a seizure before. He had a minor problem with his liver, for which he had a blood test a few months ago at his general practitioner, but he is not a drinker and is not taking any medication.

The brain scan is completely normal. I am flummoxed; this is a real mystery. I call on my favourite physician again. I start my sentence with an all too familiar, 'Hi. Can you help me with a guy in the resuscitation room. I don't know what's going on with him.' At least the midazolam has stopped the shouting.

The family asks if they can see The Shouter and, against hospital policy, I let the wife through. She reports anxiously to me that he seems very sleepy. I tell her that is because I gave him some intravenous anti-shout. I go on to say that I'm fairly sure that he has had a seizure, because his brain scan is essentially normal.

The physician, clever beast that he is, cottons on to the vague liver history and asks me to run a blood ammonia level.

'Ammonia?' I ask. 'Sure. Why?'

'Well, doctor,' he starts with a glimmer in his eye, 'I have looked up his surname on my laboratory App here,' he holds up his mobile, 'and it seems that his little liver problem is a lot more serious than his family thinks. One of the liver's jobs is to remove ammonia from the colon and make it ready to get excreted at the kidney. Liver or renal failure can result in an accumulation of ammonia, affecting the brain and giving him seizures.'

He does a pretend shrug, like I can't believe you didn't know that, and I can see that he is smiling under his mask and visor.

'You are a genius,' I tell him, and I mean it sincerely. The patient was safely home in a few days.

Forty-Two

13 July 2020

Every day, it is a personal battle for me to get out of bed and drive to the hospital.

The impulse to run away is stronger each day. South Africa is doing badly with our numbers; our rate of people testing positive per capita of population is in the top 5 in the world. Our death rate is less than Europe and the UK, but our population is much younger. The hospitals are flooded with patients and the staff is exhausted.

The responsibility weighs heavily on me and I wonder what would happen if I just resigned. No one is irreplaceable and I am sure that things would keep ticking over, but it seems like a cowardly thing to do.

Cowardly, but very appealing.

It is Monday morning and the sky is full of stars. I have pre-dawn blues and my playlist is back to Simon and Garfunkel.

My uncle died yesterday; he would have been 97 this month but he got Covid, which was probably the final straw for him. It is the end of an era. I recall him as a young man laughing with my parents and a group of friends on a Saturday night, sashaying away from the record player as 'The Girl from Ipanema' played. The last time I saw him, his hair was a bright white halo, and he had no idea who I was. It is sad how age diminishes us.

Yesterday's gruelling wind has gone, and the dawn is still and orange. It is a strange feeling that the sun comes up even when people die; that this is a sunrise and a day that they will not see.

I meet one of the remaining physicians in the corridor and she looks wrung out. She tells me that she has been working nonstop for more than 36 hours and that she cannot carry on like this. I tell her that I cannot see myself keeping up the pace either and that I am thinking of absconding.

'Really?' She asks, surprised, and with a glimmer of hope in her eyes. I can see what she's thinking behind the visor and mask. If I can do it, so can she.

I shatter the dream.

'Ethically, I don't think that we can leave, hey?'

'I suppose not.' She sounds so disappointed and I feel sorry for her. She is a tiny woman, short in stature and very slight in build and she looks like a child in a nightgown, dressed up for a pandemic. She wanders off to see the next patient and I head in the opposite direction to see my first patient.

There are only two of the six physicians in our hospital left standing. The others have Covid. So, these two are working around the clock to manage the 100 or so patients already in the wards and ICU. About 20 new COVID admissions come in every day, along with the regular patients. Three to five deaths a day. We are a relatively small hospital with only 263 beds. Anyone can see that this equation cannot work out.

There is great consternation in the private sector that the government services will try to dump their extra case load on the private sector. There are discussions about daily rates in ICU and how lean the cut can be. One and all with whom I have spoken say they are prepared to see Covid patients now for free, given the pandemic. But they will not accept any payment that will compromise their position if a National Health Service were to be introduced. Most doctors will help if they can, but they will not be owned by a corrupt government. They are adamant that they would rather leave medicine. I have to say that I agree with this sentiment and it leaves me in limbo as regards the future of medicine in South Africa.

Last night, the president announced an immediate ban on the sale of alcohol and a curfew from nine in the evening to four in the morning. I suppose that this is a good thing. The sale of cigarettes has been banned from the beginning of the first lockdown and I certainly think that, for the people directly around you, alcohol is more dangerous than smoking. I cannot see how a person smoking in a suburb across the city will directly affect me, but that same person driving drunk may very well have an impact, so to speak. The curfew may also help with the spiralling crime rate which has always been a problem in South Africa.

From my years working in The Pit at Baragwanath and in ED in the private sector, there is no doubt that alcohol and trauma are bedfellows.

There are always files waiting and I never seem to get on top of them. I really do wish that I could give notice. I feel like I have done my bit. I look at the calendar. I have been doing this for over four months.

I want to quit.

Forty-Three

I nitially I thought that my story would end when the pandemic was over. Now I know that this craziness is not likely to be over any time soon. I was hoping for a happy ending; that it wouldn't be as bad as we feared and that we would cruise through the finish line with no deaths and plenty of energy in hand.

Now it seems that there will be no finish line. We have had too many deaths to recall individual patients. My world seems devoid of energy and happiness. I can't remember the last time that I really laughed, except for dark humour meant to blunt the sharp tragedy of my everyday work.

A return to normality is about as likely as winning the lottery. Our doctors' room is piled high with boxes and boxes of death certificates. There are flies peppering the containers outside and the black frost has killed all the plants in the parking lot. The generator drones on day and night because the national power utility keeps cutting off the electricity.

Life seems pretty bleak and the alternative, even bleaker.

I did entertain the possibility that I would die of Covid before I finished writing the book. That may still happen. But what I did not consider is that this virus would poison my relationship with medicine and damage it so deeply.

I have always worked hard in the ED. Sixty to eighty hours a week is routine and, although I have seen burnout in my colleagues, I have never felt over stretched. I have had bad days, of course. Bad

207

weeks even. But I have never woken up every morning and dreaded the day ahead as I do now. I have never had to force myself to go into the rooms and examine the patients. I am tired of shouting through masks and the chaos that has become my everyday reality.

This morning I open a side ward door in order to use the room for a consultation. The file is in my hand and the patient is following hot on my heels.

There is a dead body lying on the bed.

I immediately close the door, with an 'Oops' under my breath and take the patient to another room.

When I am finished with the consult, I go to the unit manager. I lean on her door jamb and ask her if she knows about the dead body in room five. She looks surprised. We go to the room together.

There is a blue duvet under the patient which was obviously brought from home. There is a lot of blood on his chest and abdomen. It turns out that he was shot in a robbery at his home a day ago and declared dead on arrival at the ED. The staff was so busy that they forgot to do the correct notifications.

They have forgotten a dead body in a cubicle for a whole day. There is something so dreadful about this, so crazy, that it stops me in my tracks.

I turn to the unit manager. She has been my friend and colleague for almost 30 years.

'I'm not sure how much more of this I can bear.' I say simply. 'You and I are the last two standing.' We are the only two faces in ED that have been here from the beginning; we are the hands pulling the patients across from the stretchers and connecting them to oxygen. We are the eyes, the only part of us visible; we are the voices on the telephone, trying to make plans and compromises and not turn anyone away.

'I want to run away,' I tell her, 'but I can't leave. It's not in my nature. Maybe I'm a fighter. Maybe I'm just stubborn. It is like a doggedness, a determination welling up from my mind and my heart that probably would have made me a good soldier. But I didn't sign up for a war. I knew medicine could be hazardous, but this,' I wave my hand towards the patients labouring to breathe, the queue of ambulances trying to offload their stretchers and the little huddles of family members dotted about the car park, 'I didn't sign up for this.'

It is probably the most heartfelt expression of sentiment that the unit manager has ever heard from me. We are friends, but seldom discuss anything profound. Our days are too busy for deep and meaningful moments.

I can see that she is exhausted too. We have both lost weight – the pandemic is starting to shred our minds and bodies. Her blue eyes are watery and slightly vacant, and she scans the corridors and cubicles constantly vigilant for problems in the making. Her hat sits at a crazy angle and her gown is way too big for her.

I am not sure if I want to laugh like a crazy jackal or burst into tears.

The hospital is teetering on the verge of collapse. It is only our determination to keep going that pushes the queues, gets the patients through and finds beds when there are none. When one of us flags, the other pulls ahead.

I dip my fingers in sanitiser and touch the screen of my phone to wake it up and check the bed availability. I see that five specialists have been added to the Covid WhatsApp group. I know them individually – a gastroenterologist, two orthopods, a rheumatologist and a plastic surgeon – but I have not seen them since the start of lockdown. I wonder why they are on the group.

Within half an hour, I get the answer. The physician comes to the ED to see the new admissions, and he has the little band of specialists in tow. They have stethoscopes dug out of storage and hung around their necks, masks and visors in place. I am sure that none of them have listened to a patient's chest in more than 20 years.

'What are you guys doing here?' I ask.

'We have come to help,' the gastroenterologist answers simply.

Unexpectedly, my eyes fill with tears. So much respect, in that moment, knowing that these doctors don't have to do this. They could have stayed at home, out of the firing line, but they have courageously stepped forward to help us.

We are far enough into the pandemic to know that PPE may slow this germ down, but it is not a fail-safe measure. The coronavirus is ubiquitous; like a child using glitter at the play station. Despite all measures, a little shimmer will show up on your shoe the next day.

It is everywhere. And these five are volunteering to care for the Covid pneumonias under the supervision of the pulmonologist. They are, of course, qualified doctors. But I am sure that it is years since they made a move to save a stranger's life. Or any life, for that matter. The next few weeks will be tough for them, but I am sure they will be exhilarated and energised as well.

I take so much for granted and, like a beast of burden, sometimes the weight of responsibility chafes my skin. My colleagues joke with me that I am the only 'real' doctor that they know, and, in this moment, I see how intrinsically meaningful my average workday is.

I realise that I am exhausted, but I am not yet done.

Forty-Four

I think that we have turned the corner in terms of the coronavirus bell curve. We are not out of the woods, not by a long shot. But we have one nostril above the waterline now.

The new general surgeon offers show me a few tricks with chest drains. We are doing many more of them since the beginning of the pandemic and there must be an association between Covid and collapsed lungs. I take her up on her offer not two hours after she made it.

'I have a patient with a pneumothorax.' I WhatsApp her.

'You are kidding!' She answers immediately. 'On my way.'

She is a slight woman with small hands and so she shows me how to use the heavier instruments to get her way. She asks me where to cut. I show her the Professor's spot, just below the armpit hair.

'Not bad,' she says. 'Just a little lower and a little more forward. High is safer than low; less chance of encountering any abdominal organs by accident, but you are just a bit too high. The lung curves in from the chest wall there and you will struggle.'

I dutifully move one centimetre down and one forwards and infiltrate the area with local anaesthetic.

She cuts a hole in the chest wall and follows her deft fingers with a heavy curved artery forceps. Opening the jaws of the forceps against the resistance of the muscles in the chest wall, I see what she means by leverage. The curves of the forceps yawn ferociously

211

open, then nose further down and yawn again. I can hear the gristly sound of the intercostal muscles tearing.

No wonder she insisted that I sedate the patient deeply.

When she gets into the chest cavity, an alarming hissing sound begins. It makes me deeply anxious, as if the patient has sprung a leak and is deflating in front of me.

'Is that hissing sound, ummm, right?' I ask, resisting the impulse to put my hand over the hole.

She smiles knowingly. 'Hissing is good. Excellent, in fact. It is the trapped air escaping. Here, put your finger in. Can you feel where you are supposed to be?'

I feel around. Rib above, rib below, something bumping on the tip of my finger which I think must be his lung. I hope it isn't his liver. It is a tight, familiar plane. 'Got it.' I say.

Now I am the go-to person in the hospital for chest drains.

Watch one, do one, teach one.

The winter wind is still beastly but there is some green showing on the grass. The jasmine is in flower and the heady scent is everywhere. They have taken down one of the tents outside the ED and you can see the No Smoking sign again.

The government has finally authorised the antibody tests. They will be available in two days' time. I have been waiting for them to come out; but now that I can finally test, I have cold feet. What if I don't have any antibodies? How many antibodies will be adequate for immunity? What if I get complacent and the virus mutates?

I fear that I am already complacent. Yesterday, I needed to fetch a packet of medication from next to a patient's bed in order to write up his chronic script. He was deep in the Covid ward, but I could see the bag on his bedside table. I held my breath, ran past all the other beds, snatched the bag and carried it out into the corridor. I had already laid out paper towels on the table, so I put the bag and the contents on the towels, put on fresh gloves and made a list. Then I rolled all the empty pill boxes and blister packs up in the paper towels and tossed them in the hazardous materials bin.

Fresh gloves again and I was ready to go. Later, I confessed my deed to the Favourite Physician. He laughed and said that he also holds his breath with high risk patients.

He still got Covid.

Technically, the state of disaster ends today. I wonder what the government will do. I don't think that we are far enough out of the woods to lift all the restrictions. But the economy is teetering and many countries in Europe have gone into a second lockdown.

The South African public seems angry and directionless, which is not a good combination. I wish that we could all just get a memo that the pandemic has been cancelled with immediate effect.

Forty-Five

Another Sunday morning rolls around, and I am at my post It is still chilly, but spring is definitely coming. The sunrise is earlier, and the sunset takes just a few minutes longer to burn out in the west.

Yesterday, we saw Merle on the evening walk. She often flies overhead in big loops, cawing and gliding, but yesterday she was strangely quiet. She wheeled above our band of snoopies but she did not make a sound. As she swooped low, we saw the nick in her wing, a little gap in the feathers that told the story of her broken wing and her short stay with us. Her eye was just as beady, but she was silent because she was carrying a bunch of twigs in her beak.

Merle was making a nest. It made us feel so ridiculously happy that we laughed and cried and smoothed the silky snoopies while they gazed up at Merle with their soft almond eyes. Even the newcomers seemed to know who she was, as if she were part of the collective unconsciousness of the pack.

Last night, the president addressed the nation. With a few exceptions, most businesses will be able to open at midnight on Monday, 17 August. Again, I think it is the only decision that the government could make. It will be exciting to buy a good bottle of red wine again. It has been a long, dry stretch.

Monday is also the day of the antibody testing.

I present myself at the laboratory at six in the morning with a strange anxiety. I feel like I am writing an exam. The needle stings and I go back to my post with a little blob of cotton wool hidden beneath my sleeve.

I am washing my mug when I am joined by one of the surgeons in the tearoom.

'Have to do a procedure in the ICU.' He has never been one for over-zealous communication.

'Need some help?' I ask. He looks at me over the top of his glasses.

'Maybe' is his non-committal reply.

'Ok, well let me know. I'm the queen of ketamine.' I'm joking with him, but ten minutes later he calls my mobile.

He opens with 'About that ketamine…'

'Coming.' I reply. Damn, I don't know much about ketamine. Originally a veterinary drug, it has gained massive popularity in recent years in emergency medicine. It sedates people deeply but does not stop them breathing nor drop their blood pressure. This is excellent, because usually there is only one doctor in attendance to give the sedation and also to do whatever procedure needs to be done. With too deep a sedation, the doctor can end up running between the procedure and the patient's airway.

And killing a patient while trying to relocate their ankle is never good. In the old days we used benzodiazepines and morphine. Then we moved to propofol, a milky anaesthetic induction agent. Now ketamine is all the rage. The younger doctors call it 'special K'.

I get my phone out as I trot up the stairs to ICU and google the dose of ketamine. It says one milligram per kilogram. When I get to the patient's side, he tells me he weighs 140 kilograms. So, I need 140 milligrams.

I realise that I have forgotten my glasses and cannot read the tiny writing on the side of the ampule.

'How many milligrams per millilitre?' I ask the sister. She looks at the ampule and says, 'Fifty milligrams per millilitre.'

'Okay. We need 140 milligrams,' I say, and look ruefully at the 20-millilitre syringe. I try to draw up only 2.8 millilitres and ask the surgeon if he is ready.

We give the sedation and it works like a dream.

I am well pleased with myself for moving with the times and trying a new drug. I congratulate myself and give a glowing report to a friend, who is an anaesthetist, when I meet him in the corridor.

'I gave ketamine for the first time,' I report with glee.

'Oh good,' he says. 'I use it all the time. How much did you give?'

'2.8 millilitres.'

He wrinkles his nose. 'What, are you a homeopath?'

I look a bit alarmed. 'Well, it said 1 milligram per kilogram, and he weighs 140.'

The anaesthetist looks confused for a moment. 'But it's 10 milligrams per millilitre?'

'No, it's 50 milligram per millilitre.'

There is an awkward silence and both of our eyes and fingers fly to our phones.

'Jeepers,' he says, almost under his breath, and keeps on walking. I suppose his patients slept pretty well on five times the dose. There again, all patients under general anaesthetic stop breathing and need to be ventilated as a matter of course, so maybe anaesthetists are less jittery on the plunger.

I head back to the ED. I feel restless waiting for my blood result, and I hope that it will come out today. Now that they have taken the sample, the pending outcome has grown all-consuming in my head. It feels like a life-and-death issue, which, I suppose, is not far from the truth. But it is not the result of a biopsy or a test for cancer and I keep reminding myself to calm down.

For two days I have not had any Covid admissions. I haven't even seen patients with a sore throat or a cough. The mortality rate in ICU is still high and almost 100 per cent of patients on ventilators don't make it, but there are also a lot of patients who have recovered.

I think back on the past five months. I must have seen more than

200 confirmed cases of Covid 19 through the ED and the wards. It is just not possible that I don't have antibodies.

But maybe I have just been incredibly lucky so far. Maybe all the little viral particles rained around me and I didn't breathe any of them in. I sit on my chair and whirl it around. I stare at the clock and at the wall. I fiddle with the empty tray that is usually full of files. The ED is slow today and time is taking forever to pass.

The printer hums and clicks. I scoot over on my chair and pluck the paper off the catch tray.

I take a deep breath and look at the page.

It is a memo from the laboratory telling us that the testing for COVID antibodies has been suspended pending some paperwork from the Department of Health.

'No way,' I say to myself, shaking my head. I take a deep breath, throw the memo into the recycle bin and start to prowl the corridor looking for patients to see.

Epilogue

The antibody test is available today and I am fourth in the queue. I go back to the ED with another blob of cotton wool taped to the inside of my arm.

The app pings with my results first thing on Wednesday morning.

I have no antibodies.

'Bleh' is all I have to say when I open the result. The test must be incorrect. I work out approximately how many Covid pneumonias I have seen over the past six months. Well over 200. How is it possible that I have no immunity to this germ?

And what will I do now? I had jokingly told my family and friends that I will run away if my antibody test was negative. I would take it as a sign that I need to find a different day job. But I sit outside in the dusk and really think it through. There are so many reasons that I cannot leave. The snoopies need to eat and so do we. If I were to leave the ED, even if for only a few months, who would do my job? And I couldn't just appear again once the storm of Covid is passed and expect to be re-employed.

But the real reason that I cannot leave lies deep in my heart. There is a stubborn determination, an almost ornery mindset, that keeps me at my post. When I have worked with people who have pushed me physically or psychologically, my internal voice says, 'Think you can break me? Let's see who cracks first.' I can honestly say that this thought is unbidden, and this mindset only emerges

219

under extreme duress. Most of the time I am annoyingly even-tempered and easy going.

When activated, this intransigence is beyond my rational control. It is the small child in me, railing against an unfair world. It is my parents' legacy; they taught us to stand up for what was right no matter the consequence and to fight to the bitter end, even if it meant a sacrifice of the self.

'A coward dies a thousand times before his death, but the valiant man tastes of death but once.'

My mother loved that quote.

1 SEPTEMBER 2020

I was not sure that I would make it to the first official day of spring. It is still chilly in the mornings and evenings, but the days are longer and hotter.

A month ago, we rescued a pregnant greyhound and she had her puppies last week. Despite building her a whole whelping box in a separate room, so that she would not feel stressed by the unfamiliar pack, she broke into the bedroom to birth her pups next to our bed. She watched us trustingly as we lightly cleaned the velvety bundles of brindle and white and lined them up for her in a shiny squirming team.

There were seven babies but the last one was born dead. We networked with the farming community to find them good homes and spring day is going to be 'puppy meeting day' for the chosen five. The smallest and most timid of the litter will stay with us. He is brindle and white with black stripes and is accordingly named Tiger.

Somehow the puppies and their humans recognise each other and the meet and greet is clean and joyful. The puppies will only be ready to go in 6 weeks, but it is good to know that their homes are settled. It is months since we had guests at the farm and the mood is merry.

We have a socially distanced picnic and afterwards we take a long walk in the mild evening light. There is much consternation that I don't have antibodies, but I roll my eyes and make light of it. The acacia trees are vibrant against the burning sky and I change the subject, pointing out that the birds are building their nests high in the boughs. It means that there will be good rains this summer.

I say a silent word of thanks to the universe and accept that I will remain at my post.

There are, after all, still lives to be saved.

We thank the following for their support in publishing this book:

Arthur Goldstuck
Ashwin Moyene
Ben Williams
Beverley Naidoo
Carolyn Raphaely
Catriona Jarvis
Corinne Rosmarin
Denis Hirson
Dianne Stewart
Gill Bolton
Glen Impey
Graeme Friedman
Helen Douglas
James Bissett
Karin Pampallis

Kevin Ritchie & Associates
Louis Gaigher
Maeve King
Mamma Jacqui
Mary Burton
Michelina Giacovazzi
Moira Levy
Roger Southall
Rona V van Niekerk
Ryan Childs
Sebastian Seedorf
Steven Dubin
Sue Grant-Marshall
Trisha Cornelius